IN ALL THEIR AFFLICTION

By

Rev. Murdoch Campbell
M.A.

KNOX PRESS (EDINBURGH)
15 NORTH BANK STREET
EDINBURGH, EH1 2LS

First Edition   1967
Second Edition   1969

Printed by
JOHN G. ECCLES
Henderson Road, Longman
Inverness

Foreword

THERE are two or three remarks that I should like to make in relation to the following chapters. It may appear to some that my treatment of the subject under discussion is rather subjective and that I should have observed a more obvious balance between the inner, or experimental, side of Christian affliction and its more doctrinal or expository side. It may be seen, however, that opposite every source of sorrow on which I have touched I have, at the same time, tried to show that God's grace and healing balm are ever available and sufficient, and that in every trial His own presence and promise sweeten "the waters of Marah."

I have also introduced a few instances of the Lord giving His Word "in the night watches" and "when deep sleep falleth upon men." And in each case its relevance, and its fulfilment within the sphere of Providence, were the proof that it comes from Him who has "the tongue of the learned." It is the witness of Scripture — and also of Christian experience — that the Spirit of the Lord who dwells in the hearts of His people can apply His own Word to their mind both while they are awake and asleep.

M. C.

Contents

The Unpreached Sermon 9

Our Bethels — A Preparation 16

"The Body of this Death" 27

The Besetting Sin 37

The Fears of the Flock 45

The Great Adversary 55

"Giant Despair" 70

Loneliness 79

"The Crook in the Lot" 91

Frustration 100

Tomorrow's Care 109

Broken Ties 117

"By Babel's Streams 125

The Imperilled World 136

The Last Enemy 143

CHAPTER I.

THE UNPREACHED SERMON

IT happened one autumn evening. I was walking along a quiet road in one of our Highland glens when, all of a sudden, I felt my heart going out in much tenderness toward those of God's people whom I knew to be bowed down under burdens of sorrow and care. With my heart thus touched I found, at the same time, these words in my mind: "As the lily among the thorns, so is my love among the daughters." And I knew that these words from the lips of our Lord described, in vivid language, not only the spiritual beauty of His people in contrast to the world, but also their painful environment here. For in this world they must suffer till they reach the place where sorrow is unknown.

At that moment I prayed that I might be enabled, as God would have me, to bear their burdens and so fulfil one of the kindly laws which govern His kingdom in this world. Perhaps, I thought, I could do something to comfort them in their manifold tribulations. While life's brief candle was still burning could I not, for example, write a word in season which might, by the blessing of God, help some of them in the way?

As this somewhat wistful, but strangely compelling, thought took possession of my mind I recalled an incident which took place in my life some years before. I was sitting in my home in Glasgow, and trying to prepare a sermon which I intended to preach in one of our congregations. It was a Communion preparatory sermon. And, like a sharp blade, it was meant to cut through all the veneer of mere outward formality, and to expose the hidden evils of the hearts and lives of my hearers. It was meant to hurt and to bring those who heard it to their knees in grief and penitence for sin. Into its texture I admitted little or no comfort at all.

When I had finished my task that night I went to bed — and dreamed. I dreamt that I was standing in the open-air, and in a place of breath-taking loveliness. The earth around me was green and enriched by the rarest of flowers. Their wafted fragrance made it a joy to breathe. In this exquisite setting I saw a table at which a company of men and women sat down. They were, I knew, waiting to commemorate the death of their Lord. They also seemed to be pressed down with much sorrow, as if they all felt the plague of sin which lodged in their hearts. At the end of this table I stood, but I knew not what to say. It was then that I saw a man walking toward me who said in a calm voice that I should address the waiting company.

"And what shall I say?" I asked him.

"There is," he said, "but one thing to say here." Then, in a voice laden with tenderness and affection, he quoted the words of Isaiah: " 'Comfort ye, comfort ye my people, saith your God. Speak ye comfortably to Jerusalem, and cry unto her, that her warfare is accomplished, that her iniquity is pardoned: for she hath received of the Lord's hand double for all her sin.' "

When I awoke that morning I decided that I should leave it to others to proclaim the word of severity, and that in addressing God's people during that Communion season God would have me apply His balm to their wounds.

Remembering that morning, and before I had reached the end of the road, the conviction formed itself in my mind that, with God's help, I should continue this ministry in comfort. It was impressed on my heart that one great end of our calling is to comfort the people of God. The supreme evidence of our love for Christ is that we feed, and care for, His flock. He is so identified with them that in ministering to them we minister to Himself. This, often unconscious, service of our love to Him is what He will one day acknowledge and reward. But as I came to the end of the way, I was confronted with a very difficult question. Had I the needed personal fitness for this task? Did my own experience — for what it is worth — provide me with even the minimum qualifications to deal with the delicate subject of Christian sorrow and consolation?

And here, indeed, I ought to offer some explanation. During the first years of my Christian life God was pleased to shelter me from almost every storm. The harrowing conviction of sin through which the Lord, I trust, led me into a state of grace gave way to a great peace. I was spiritually but a child then. I was like one whom the Lord carried in His bosom and led gently in green pastures and by quiet streams. Under His shadow I sat down enjoying rest of soul. He restrained every foe. If the devil roared, it was from afar. The dogs which sometimes barked and bared their teeth were not permitted to hurt me. My sky was bright, like a morning without cloud. In Scripture, and in Christian biography, I read of the dark folds which so often enclose and distress God's people. The path of anguish of which

David, Asaph and Heman speak in the Psalms, my feet
had not yet touched. No doubt when I did touch on the
subject of Christian affliction my words were scriptural
and, perhaps, helpful to some; but into these deep waters
I had not yet come.

But the day of trouble did arrive. The sky which was
hitherto so bright above me began to darken till every
star vanished behind dark and heavy clouds of fear and
spiritual conflicts. This contact with adversity was not
something which passed in a day or a year. Although
some of its earlier tossings may have spent their force
the wind is still oftentimes contrary. And this, no doubt,
is how it will fare with me — as with so many of God's
people — until, by God's grace, I come into the deep
calm and perfect peace of the eternal world. I hope,
therefore, that in trying to comfort and reassure God's
afflicted people I am not altogether a stranger to the
inevitable and necessary trials which, for His glory and
their own good, they are called upon to endure in this
life.

At this point, however, let me introduce a needed
word of caution. We live in the age of the false prophet,
one of whose works is to place soft deceptive pillows
under the heads of men and women who know not the
Lord, and who are, therefore, strangers to "the afflictions
of Joseph." These men echo their ancient counterparts
whose favourite cry was — "Peace, peace." They excel
in ministering what they call "uplifts" to those who listen
to them. With that one word they lull them into a fatal
sleep of spiritual unconcern. Whatever we are, and however we live, we are, according to these men, within the
circle of God's love and therefore entitled to His
consolation. From this confusion we turn away as from

something which is both unscriptural and abhorrent to the Christian mind. It is a confusion which is also abhorred of God, as His Word so clearly reveals.

As a safeguard against this error we ought at the outset to ask ourselves a question. How can we identify God's people in this world? Fortunately for us God Himself gives us a very full and inerrant picture of His Own children, and those who answer to the Scriptural characteristics He sets before us are truly His. We are not, therefore, dependent on man's judgment in this matter — if that judgment is not in harmony with God's voice in His written Word.

In the light of Scripture God's people are to be identified as those who are renewed by the Holy Spirit, who are washed in the blood of Christ from sin's guilt and defilement, who have renounced their own righteousness that they might be clothed in His, and in whose renewed hearts a new love is born. This love rests on Himself, on His Word and on His people. And with this love is an evergrowing desire after holiness of life — a desire which, in the words of the Psalm, God is going to accomplish.

Our Lord further describes His Own people as His sheep for whom He died and to whom he gives eternal life. This name, although figurative, is also highly significant and full of instruction. His sheep bear His Own mark and seal. An older generation of Christians used to enlarge on this pleasant theme. Christ's flock, they used to say, have His mark and seal both in the wool and in the ear. The mark in the wool is more conspicuous, and may be seen by all. The believer, in other words, reveals by his outward conduct Whose he is and Whom he serves. There is also a secret seal —

they all have the hearing ear. They know and hear His voice, and what He commands they seek to do. In their worship, and in their inner and outward conduct, they seek to be ruled by His will as it is revealed in His Word.

They walk, in other words, in "the footsteps of the flock," or in those holy paths which were loved and cherished by God's people in every age. In His pastures they also feed. God's Word is their spiritual food, and at the Throne of Grace, in communion with their Lord, they drink out of living streams. They refuse to defile their lips with any fare but that which He has provided for them in the Gospel. Their eye, also, is on the Shepherd. He is their Example and Guide. He is the end of their conversation and desire. When they lose sight of Him they mourn, but His hiding is only for a moment. They know His care and love. When they are weary and feeble He leads them gently and bears them in His arms. And because they love Him, they are hated of all men. "For his sake they are killed all the day long: they are counted as sheep for the slaughter" (Psalm 44). They are therefore commanded by their Lord to "beware of dogs" that would hurt and pursue them.

They are a people, too, who see the Lord's love for them in His chastisements. When they go out of the way they come under His rod, and that is how He often conveys His higher lessons to their souls. They have "no fellowship with the unfruitful works of darkness." They are a people apart. In their holy attachments they are like sheep and doves. Christ uses both figures to describe them. When clouds and darkness descend upon them, and when their souls are discouraged in the way, they long for the rest of Heaven, and for that country where the inhabitant shall not say, "I am sick."

There are other figures which the Bible employs to describe them. They are the light of the world and the salt of the earth. In their warfare against evil they employ the whole armour of God. They are not a passive, timid people where the glory of God is concerned. They go forth against the forces of darkness in the name of Him who, as the Captain of their salvation, goes forth "conquering and to conquer." The Church, with God within her and around her, has been "a terror" to Satan and wicked men in every age. Hell has often trembled before her who is "terrible as an army with banners."

This subject, however, is too rich and inexhaustible; for a perfect picture of the Lord's people is outwith our power to produce here. "It doth not yet appear what we shall be"; but what we have said, based on Christ's Own words, should enable us at least to identify them as "not of this world," but as truly His.

The following pages are, therefore, meant for those who bear His mark and who enjoy the earnest of good things to come in their hearts. And the comfort we would minister to them is, we hope, that comfort wherewith we ourselves are comforted of God.

CHAPTER II.

OUR BETHELS — A PREPARATION

THERE are some who draw a picture of the Christian life as one of undisturbed quiet and unfailing joy, and from which conflict and adversity are almost absent. But the voyage to Heaven is not always on such a tranquil sea.

Christ in His parable of the sower tells us of a spurious type of conversion which consists of a mere flash of emotional joy, but which fades away with its first contact with trial. Bunyan's "Pliable" ran toward Heaven when he heard of its glories and rewards; but with his first encounter with adversity he ran even faster in the opposite way. Certain forms of modern preaching too often picture the Christian life as without cross or burden. And many take the bait only to find that, without persevering grace in the heart, their hopeful beginnings die under the first shock of temptation. It is this absence of grace, and the neglect of counting the cost, which cause the great majority of those who apparently "receive the word" to go back and follow the Lord no more.

Certainly there are within the context of true Christian experience perfect peace and unspeakable joy. But there is something else. There is sin and therefore there is sorrow and continuous warfare. The heavenly wayfarers' path to Heaven lies through dark vales where enemies prowl and try — if that were possible — to destroy them.

In the New Testament we see the wisdom of the Lord in the way He warns all true believers with regard to the implications and commitments of the Christian life. There is no belittlement of what is in store for those who renounce the world, forsake the Devil's camp, and so wage a daily warfare against sin. "Beloved, think it not strange concerning the fiery trial which is to try you, as though some strange thing happened unto you" (I. Peter 4: 12): "for we wrestle not against flesh and blood, but against principalities, against powers, against the rulers of the darkness of this world, against spiritual wickedness in high places" (Ephesians 6: 12). And to be forewarned is to be forearmed.

The young Christian, especially, is sometimes in danger of envisaging a calm and happy future in keeping with his first spiritual enjoyments. Job did this. He was to die in his nest, with God's secret upon his tabernacle, and his faith in God wrapped up in peace to the end. He had, as yet, no awareness that the hateful eyes of Satan were upon him, and that "he desired to have him that he might sift him as wheat."

David, too, thought that his "mountain" would stand strong and remain unclouded to the end; but before long, with God's face withdrawn, sorrow and fear filled his heart.

There are many illustrations both in Scripture and in Christian biography of this season of quiet rest before the disciplines which God so often uses for our spiritual profit and refinement.

But the day will come when, through steep and thorny paths, and beneath terrifying precipices, we haltingly follow Him. The blessedness we enjoyed when first we knew Him becomes a wistful memory. The Prophet speaks of this in his parable of the infant in the field. He gives us a picture of the Church in the first season of her spiritual marriage, before the days of darkness had arrived. "And when I passed by thee I said unto thee, Live, and thy time was the time of love . . . . and thou becamest mine" (Ezekiel 16). Was this not a picture of Israel when they stood on the further shore of the sea with all their enemies lying in the silence of death? There they sang for joy. The days of their mourning had ended. By the sprinkling of the blood of the Covenant, and by the exertion of God's power they were free. Elim with its palm trees and refreshing springs now gladdened their souls. But Elim was not Canaan. Between them and the place of rest lay "the great and terrible wilderness" where God was to try their faith and search their hearts.

The story is told of a young man who entered into peace with God. But his day of spiritual calm came to an end. Sin began to rear its ugly head within his soul. What did it mean? Was he really a converted man? He decided to consult an older Christian man about his fears. Before, however, he had time to unfold his distress, his friend greeted him with the words, "So, I hear you are called up to the war." He then understood that God had called him, not only to Himself, but to wage war with Satan and sin.

Let not the young in grace be discouraged, then, if after solid tokens of the Lord's love they are led to endure hard things. Our Lord Himself, speaking with all reverence, had His hour of holy calm before His feet touched the path of tribulation. At the Jordan God proclaimed His pleasure in Him, while the Holy Spirit rested on Him in the form of a dove; but from that quiet scene He was led to wage war with the powers of evil and to endure temptations which, in their unknown depth, have no parallel in mere human experience.

One reason why God's hand may be so bountiful toward us at the beginning of our Christian life is that in remembering His goodness we might not faint in the way. God said to the Prophet, "Arise and eat; because the journey is too great for thee." And in the strength of that great blessing he covered the long road between Dan and Beersheba.

For example, the Lord knew all the trials and frustrations which Jacob must endure for twenty years in Padan-aram. But before the stress of that long period, He made him lodge with Him one night in Heaven, and gave him a blessing that sustained his hope through all his days. It was a night which Jacob shall remember, we believe, throughout eternity. At Bethel God's blissful Presence filled his soul. "Surely the Lord is in this place . . . . this is none other but the house of God, and this is the gate of Heaven." His wonderful and meaningful dream brought him much nearer to the bliss and reality of eternity than any other event in his life. That treasured hour ever afterwards served as a fond link between his soul and God. The God of Bethel was his God for evermore. But that lovely dawn was but a prelude to a long day of sorrow.

The same could be said also of Paul. It was some time after his conversion that he was favoured with great nearness to God. How it happened he did not know. Whether he was "in the body or out of the body" he

could not tell. In a moment he found himself in "the
third heaven," that is, in the higher dimension of the
eternal world.

The Hebrews sometimes spoke of three heavens. The
first is the place immediately about us — where the birds
sing. The next is the awesome astronomical heavens
which form the universe. The third is the glorious place
beyond, or the "City of the Great King." There Paul
saw and heard things which no pen or tongue of man
could describe. And ever after that day he makes little
of his sufferings in the service of his Lord. In one place
he presents us with an appalling catalogue of his many
trials. But not one syllable of complaint ever fell from
his lips! "I have learned, in whatsoever state I am,
therewith to be content." He made light of all, knowing
that eternal happiness with Christ in Heaven — of which
he enjoyed such a rich foretaste — would not only
enhance his reward but would also more than compensate
for all he had to endure in this lower vale.

As it was in the lives of God's people in other days,
so it is now. Let me give but one example. It is that of
a young man who was one of my dear companions on
earth. This young man could be seen walking on a
summer day on a Hebridean moor. He was accompanied
by a friend. Sometimes he would stoop down to pick
one of those rare and heather-scented flowers which, in
early June, delight and surprise those who know the
island moorlands. With each flower that met his eye he
would exclaim in near ecstasy: "How lovely He must
be Who created these, and Who has done all things well!"
This was not a mere artistic appreciation of Nature in one
of her colourful and fragrant robes, but the welling up
in his soul of a deep love of Christ Who had, a few days

before, forgiven him his sins and rescued his soul from spiritual death and despair. In his pre-converted days this young man wandered into the dark shadows of atheism and unbelief, till at last he felt like one imprisoned in a silent meaningless universe. Then one night, as he listened to a neighbour singing a Psalm, he felt himself, as by an omnipotent hand, brought out of darkness into the marvellous light of the Gospel. God broke through every barrier and embraced his soul in love and tenderness. In a moment, with his inner eyes unveiled, he could see it all. Christ had taken his place on the Tree. He died that he might live. His sin was put away "as far as east is distant from the west." Now he saw himself, not in a lonely universe without a purpose or without a God, but enjoying the presence of the One Whose existence he had so often doubted, and "accepted in the Beloved." That night a new love was born in his heart for the One Who loved him. That was why he loved even the flowers which He had made. They were speaking to him of a lovelier flower by far — "the Rose of Sharon and the Lily of the Valleys."

But his happy spiritual morning was soon followed by deep and prolonged spiritual conflicts. He went to Heaven on a stormy sea. But Christ's promises to his soul, along with a treasured assurance of His love, and a foretaste of the joys reserved for him in a better world, sustained and supported him to the end. With Paul he could say: "I know whom I have believed, and am persuaded that he is able to keep that which I have committed unto him against that day."

As a fit comment on this story I should like to quote the words of a Christian man who had for many years been a follower of the Lord. This man once found himself in the company of several young believers. A young woman, who had but recently "tasted that the Lord is gracious" was telling the story of her new-found joy, and of that love "which is better than wine." It was the love of Christ shed abroad in her heart that caused her lips to speak. When she had finished her story her older friend said in a quiet voice, "Drink your wine, my dear, while you may: the waters of Marah you will reach soon enough."

These remarks may serve to show that before God places us under our several burdens and crosses He often gives us solid tokens of His love and care. We must not, therefore, be discouraged if, after a morning of joy, much of life's brief day may be laden with heavy clouds. But through these clouds many rays of comfort often break through. They are the tokens that our times are in His hands, and that behind these clouds the sun of His love is for ever shining.

Whatever sorrows may touch the life of God's people in this world their joy in the Lord, consciously or unconsciously, remains with them. Paul was exceeding joyful in all his tribulations. Those who, on the other hand, say that God's people should dismiss all sorrow from their lives speak contrary to Christian experience in every age and to God's purpose for them in this life. It is out of the womb of sorrow that many of their future and endless joys are going to emerge. In that day their sorrow and sighing shall give place to joy and gladness.

While the Lord's people should never deliberately conceal their spiritual joy from an unbelieving world they should, on the other hand, be careful against disclosing their peculiar sorrows to those who are strangers to these. One thing which greatly impressed the pagan world of the apostolic age was the joy of those whom the glad tidings of the Gospel had drawn to Christ. The shout of a King was among them. They were like those who had found great spoil. This is what we often lack today. How "joy unspeakable and full of glory" can dwell at the same time in a broken and a contrite heart is, of course, one of the paradoxes of the true Christian life. It is, however, something which is very real to all who know the Lord. And the one cannot bear comparison with the other! The one is momentary and light while the other has its source in our everlasting communion with God. It was a frequent remark of Dr John Duncan that the sighs of the Church of God were infinitely preferable to the so-called pleasures of the world. Moses, to use but one example, had more joy in sharing the afflictions of the people of God for a season than he would have with all the riches, honours and pleasure of Egypt in his possession. While we therefore mention some of the sorrows of the Lord's people we know that beyond and greater than all these is the joy which by the Spirit of God, is sown in their heart.

But the heights and depths of the Christian life are not the real evidence of its existence; but rather our sense of need bringing us daily to the Lord for the needed strength. And as the Christian life — however normal its complexion — is never free from pain, God's ministry of grace is continuous. And no trial shall ever emerge in our life, but His grace is sufficient for us; and He is there with the grace that He gives.

We should also remember that chastisement, whatever form it may take in the life of each one of us, is a fundamental implication of our relationship to God. "You only have I known of all the families of the earth, therefore I will punish you for all your iniquities." "For whom the Lord loveth he chasteneth and scourgeth every son whom he receiveth."

Not long ago I met an excellent Christian man who, in the days of his youth, "sat under" a well-known minister — the Rev. George MacKay of Fearn in Ross-shire. Out of the treasures of his memory this man brough forth some rare saying of this herald of the Good Tidings. One of these was on the love of God in His chastisements upon his own children. The preacher illus-trated his theme. He recalled the old Highland days when a wise and affectionate father would have the little domestic "strap" suspended on a nail by the fireside in his home. It was there, more or less, as a reminder that any serious form of misbehaviour on the part of his children, either in words or deeds, might bring them under correction. He loved his children, and he would therefore, if need be, exercise the appropriate discipline which would ensure their safety, their moral welfare, and a becoming conduct. In the same way, said the preacher, "the Lord has the rod of His chastisement suspended by the fire of His eternal love in His covenant Home," and when His children, in heart or in walk, go against His will He will use it for their good. "Foolishness is bound in the heart of a child, but the rod of correction shall drive it far from him." As long as we are in this vale we remain as children both in knowledge and wisdom. Not till we enter Heaven shall we come to the stature of the perfect man. Though we grow in grace and in knowledge the follies and limitation of children cling to us here. Besides, before God called us into His grace, and adopted us into His own family, we were the children of wrath even as others. And do not the marks and habits of our former life sometimes mar, and cast their shadow, over our Christian life and witness? It was an apt saying of the famous Alexander Gair that although God took the Children of Israel out of Egypt in one night it took Him forty years to take Egypt out of them. Their murmurings, indiscretions and rebellions had their roots in their own sinful and often foolish hearts. Therefore God's chastisement followed them throughout their long pilgrimage. He loved them. He pitied them "as a father pitieth his children." He kept pace with their slow and uncertain progress. By the rod of correction He often withdrew them from their purpose and folly. His unchanging love for them was often and necessarily wrapped in pain.

If many of God's dealings with us here are mysterious, the day is coming when all shall be made plain. "In that day," says Christ, "ye shall ask me nothing." How beautifully is this expressed in the verse:

"Not till the loom is silent,
    And the shuttles cease to fly —
Will God unroll the pattern,
    And explain the reason why:
The dark threads are as needful
    In the weaver's skilful hand,
As the thread of gold and silver
    For the pattern He has planned."

It were well for us also to remember that only through affliction and chastisement do we come to know something of the Divine Compassion, or of the depth of pity and love which dwells in the heart of Christ toward His own. It can never be discovered otherwise. We can but faintly know the love which dwells in the heart of a mother or a friend till we are touched by affliction. But human sympathy is but a feeble reflection of the love of Him who was born for adversity, and "who makes all our bed in our sickness." "Lord, he whom thou lovest is sick." These were the words which touched the heart of our Lord on earth, and brought Him to Martha's and Mary's side in the day of their grief. It was in the hour of their sorrow that they saw something of the unspeakable love which lodged in His soul. "Jesus wept." "Behold, how He loved him." "In all their affliction He was afflicted." This is, indeed, a discovery that shall endear Him to us, beyond all that tongue can tell, throughout eternal ages.

It was my deep affection for these words of the Prophet that compelled me to use them as a title for my little work. They are words which, on innumerable occasions, have served as a well of indescribable consolation to my spirit.

CHAPTER III.

" THE BODY OF THIS DEATH "

IN coming nearer to our subject we may begin at the very centre of the Christian life and then move towards its wider circumference. We would like, first of all, to deal with those inward conflicts which are peculiar to Christian experience and the source of which may not lie in any external circumstances. There are hidden sorrows which may persist and deepen throughout one's life while in our outward lot we may be free from much care. If such grief lies within our hearts it might be helpful to enquire as to its cause. If, as we have said, the time of our "first love" is often one of much peace it may also be a time when we may nurse the fond illusion that sin is for ever slain in our soul. But we soon discover that although God has for ever put our sin away in its dominion, guilt and penal nature, its presence in the soul is still a terrible reality. It is crucified, but not dead. The serpent's head is bruised, but its tireless enmity remains.

This conflict within the new-born soul is the evidence of our new nature. With the life and love of God now "shed abroad in our hearts" the desire to do the will of God is present with us. The true Christian, in the words of Dr John Duncan, is therefore "a complex man" in whose soul two opposite laws are at war. He is a new man in whose inner life the old law of sin and the new law of grace strive for the mastery. These laws — the one written by Satan's finger in our Fall, and the other by God in our regeneration — are mutually hostile. This warfare ends only when we end our pilgrimage here.

The figure which Paul uses to describe this inward sense of sin which so often burdened his own soul is, "the body of this death." Even if, as some believe, this phrase refers also to the physical body, we know that what wrung this cry from the heart of Paul was the oppressive nature and increasing motions of inward sin.

Some of his Christian readers in Rome might have understood the background to this terrible phrase. They might have heard of the inhuman tyrant who sometimes compelled his victims to walk under the weight of a dead body. To Paul, as a new man in Christ Jesus, inward sin, in all its corrupt nature, was a burden which he knew would cling to him as long as he was "in this tabernacle."

There may be deceptive seasons in the life of God's people when they may think that they have finally succeeded in burying "the old man of sin" for ever in a grave, and when they resolve to sin no more. But they soon discover that his burials are always followed by a resurrection. Their seasons of quiet are often a prelude to greater conflicts and deeper discoveries of the evil within. Perhaps at such times their greatest fear is that no true work of grace was ever wrought in their soul. Could such a plague really cling to a heart renewed by the Spirit of God? But this is a fear which has oppressed God's people in every age. This "plague of the heart," with all its dark symptoms, often makes us long for the day when it shall trouble us no more.

David Brainerd tells of an Indian woman who had enjoyed many rich tokens of God's goodness shortly after her conversion. All that she then desired was that she might live wholly to God's glory and do His Will. But sin stood in the way. One day, with tears in her eyes, she said to a friend, "I want to die — that I may sin no more."

During the great evangelical revival which swept over the North of Scotland more than a century ago, a man could now live an holy life, free from the evil thoughts which God had so richly blessed him. God had forgiven him his sins, and had cast them into the depths of the sea. A new desire was now born in his heart. If he could not live an holy life, free from the evil thoughts which so often distressed his mind, how happy he would be! It so happened that at that very time many were leaving their native land to settle down in foreign climes. Perhaps, he thought, if he emigrated with his friends, the sins which so much grieved him on his native heath might not be able to follow him to the distant places of the earth! How could they cross the great sea! In due course he arrived in the interior of Canada. One day he was present at a meeting at which he was asked to pray. But his prayer was bathed in tears. The sins from which he had fled were still with him. The simple-minded but godly man, at whose psychological innocence we may smile, then knew that the sins which distressed him in his native land had their dwelling-place in his own heart. He had learned that the burden of his sinful self he must carry with him all his days. How he would have agreed with the one who once said, "I run away from sin; but sin does not run away from me."

But why, we ask, is sin so active in every true child

of God? What accounts for this unceasing spiritual warfare in our members? The answer is that the conflict is between two irreconcileable powers which can never agree. For this we need not look. Satan and sin resent, so to speak, taking "a second place" in the spiritual home which was once all their own. Now, with their dominion broken, they are driven into a lower place, while grace has taken over the whole man, and Christ, accepted as King, is on the throne of the heart. This is what riles the devil and explains his enmity. His old haunt has been invaded by Another Who is stronger than he, and is being renewed and sanctified for God to dwell in for ever. And if he cannot hope to retain his ancient rule and sway he can, with the help of sin — his own brat — make our pillow an uneasy one here.

Now, the implications of this conflict should fill us with comfort and hope, for they go to prove that we are not now what we once were. Do we not remember the day when the presence of inward sin gave us no pain? We were dead to God, and sin, therefore, reigned in our hearts. We followed its bias and it, therefore, had no quarrel with us. We were at peace with our adversary. We were in a grave of trespass and sin. We knew nothing of our plight, or if in theory we did, it gave us no real concern.

But when in a day of God's power we were awakened by the Holy Spirit, and when that Spirit entered our souls with the brightly-lit lamp of God's Law, we began to realise where and how we were. In ourselves we "received the sentence of death" that our hope might not be any more "in ourselves but in God Who raiseth the dead." When the Law of God threw its searching beams into our heart we began to see sin in its true nature and to feel the enmity it bears to God and to all that is of God. Now, our pain at its presence within us, as that loathsome thing which God hates and which works in opposition to His Will which we love, is a proof that we live. When Paul was clad in the garments of spiritual death, self-righteousness and pride, sin gave him no grief. Others were sinners, but not he. But in a state of grace he became, in his very consciousness and recollection, "the chief of sinners." Although free from all condemnation because he was "accepted in the Beloved," and although rejoicing in Christ Jesus as his Righteousness, he grieved over sin to the very end. It was as a new creature in Christ that the cry was born in his heart — "Who shall deliver me?" It was a cry which, paradoxically enough, proclaimed that he had been delivered and that life eternal was now his. Those who have this cry in their heart, are, therefore, in good company. The unrenewed mind welcomes sin and embraces it, but the chaste and renewed soul cries to God for deliverance.

To use an illustration, there was a law in Israel that the woman who cried out in the presence of moral danger must be deemed innocent and chaste; but the one who acquiesced in the unclean act must be reckoned guilty and impure. In the same way the spiritual mind, while invaded by evil thoughts and imaginations, cries to God for deliverance, while the carnal mind lies still and is silent. Sin is, therefore, what God's people loathe and fear. They fear it as they see its dread consequences in the external world, but the sin which they discover in their own heart they fear still more. Each of them knows the heart is "desperately wicked" above every reflection of it in the world around them.

We once knew a man who in his youth worked in one

of our cities. He was brought up in a community where silly but somewhat weird "ghost" stories were often told. These nocturnal apparitions, which some were supposed to have seen, brought fear to some hearts. One day, in the city of Glasgow, he found himself sitting in a church and listening to a faithful preacher of the Gospel. In his sermon, the minister referred to the superstitious person who would tremble if he saw a so-called ghost, but to whom the destructive power of evil in his own soul gave little or no concern; and he went on to say that those who belonged to God were more afraid of one sinful thought than of every ghost in the land — even supposing they were there to be seen! To this lad this saying was a great mystery. The day came however, when God convinced him of his sin and when he knew how true the words of God's servant were.

And here we may say that our sympathy with the people of God who mourn over the evil of their hearts is a solid evidence that we are one of their number.

Many years ago in the North of Scotland a company of men were crossing a moor on the way to communion services. The way was long, and to beguile the time and to edify one another, it was proposed by one of the company that each should tell what, in the first instance, led him into the company of God's people. Each man made his own valued contribution to this tender theme. The young man who was the last to speak told of the time when he became so aware of the evil of his heart that he was afraid to go near God's people lest his very breath would contaminate their chaste conversation in Christ. He looked upon them as a people holy in heart, thought and desire, while he himself was daily oppressed with a heart laden with sin. When, however, he began to listen to their conversation, he was astonished to find that they all sorrowed over the sin which so often and so easily beset them, and were sinners like himself. This discovery awakened a love and a sympathy in his heart toward them which he knew would never die. Is it not a source of comfort to know that we are of those who "like doves of the valleys mourn every one for his iniquity"?

A woman was one day sitting in a church listening to a minister who apparently knew little of these inward conflicts. She was a choice believer. She belonged to the number whom the Lord pronounced blessed because they mourn. After the service, when comment went round about the "nice" sermon the minister had preached, she remarked: "It may be as you say, but there are dark dungeons in my heart of which evidently he knows nothing." God had broken her heart, and she therefore knew something of the kind of heart she had. She also knew of a Physician who would heal her. And for that reason she was often at His door for help.

Contrary to what some may say, our sense of inward sin does not diminish with the years. As we grow in holiness our sins loom larger and become more oppressive. As we grow in grace our conscience becomes more tender, and our mind more sensitive to the sins which lodge within. "How is it that the sins which yesterday looked like mere mole-hills appear like mountains today?" The man who once asked this question in our hearing had been for fifty years professing the Lord. How often are we overcome with shame as we view our life in retrospect? The sins of which we made merry in our unregenerate days now grieve us, while we mourn over the years which the locusts have eaten. With David we pray:

> "My sins and faults of youth
>   do Thou, O Lord, forget;
> After Thy mercy think on me,
>   and for Thy goodness great."

The greatest comfort of God's people, however, is that which is related to their hope. This made Paul cry, "I thank God through Jesus Christ, our Lord." It was a cry of triumph. That hope derives its very existence from the actual and promised perfection of God's work for them and in them. The finished work of Christ, their eternal union with Him, their justification through the imputation of His righteousness and the efficacy of His precious blood, are the sure guarantee of their final deliverance from evil. To many choice saints the most wonderful and the most endearing word in the whole Bible is that which speaks of the infinite efficacy of Christ's blood. "The blood of Jesus Christ His Son cleanseth us from **all** sin." Sin and Satan may often whisper that we have sins of thought and imagination which God cannot forgive and which His blood cannot cleanse. Our sins have passed the limits of His mercy, and are outwith the category of those which His blood can cover and remove! But, Oh, what a sword is this with which to vanquish every foe — "From **all** sin."

I was but a mere boy at the time, and I cannot now recollect how I found myself, with several companions, at a cottage meeting in a neighbour's house. But there we sat listening to the lovely singing of the Psalms, and to the prayers which were being offered by men who knew the way to the Throne of Grace. An old man stood up to pray, and in his prayer he touched on his own state and that of his friends — with all their backslidings of heart and life. It was then that a deep sob arrested his words. The long insufferable silence which followed at last ended, and in a voice which seemed to be drowned in grief he repeated the words, "The blood, Eternal One, the blood .... the blood, the blood ...." Had the Lamb Who is in the midst of the Throne not died on the Cross, his hope would have perished. But at the place where Christ died under the weight of His sins, there he could leave his burden and breathe in hope. Christ's death was His death of His people. He is also their Resurrection and their Life. "Who of God is made unto us wisdom, and righteousness, and sanctification, and redemption."

Besides all this, the sanctification of our soul is the work of the Holy Spirit. As God the Son put away sin by the sacrifice of Himself, so the Holy Spirit, Who is God, shall bring His own work to perfection. "He Who hath begun a good work in you will perform it till the day of Jesus Christ." Our deliverance from inward evil is not left to any grace or influence, apart from the One Who has in Himself infinite power and Who can, in all its fulness, apply the purchased redemption to our beings. Besides, the implication of our eternal union with Christ is that sins' ties shall all be broken. We shall all come to the glorious liberty of the children of God.

This then, is the reason why we are commanded to hope to the end, and to comfort ourselves in the Lord. This good hope through grace should, therefore, fill us with strong consolation. If original sin was the first to enter the soul, and is the last to depart it, it is good, on the other hand, to envisage the day when it shall leave us to grieve us no more.

"Let Israel hope in the Lord: for with the Lord there is mercy, and with him is plenteous redemption, And he shall redeem Israel from all his iniquities." — (Psalm 130, vv. 7-8.)

CHAPTER IV.

THE BESETTING SIN

MOST Christian people, I suppose, are afflicted with some one persistent infirmity or sin against which they must be constantly on their guard. There is a point at which we are all weak and at which, without watchfulness, our spiritual defences break down. In the life of each believer some sin stands out like the giant Goliath among the Philistine host. The dispositional infirmities which to some are a daily cross seldom trouble others. Where the one is weak, the other is strong. But no man is strong at every point of his nature, and the devil knows where the door is ajar. His snares are always set where our feet are apt to go astray.

Some choice Christian men and women are afflicted, for example, with unstable tempers. They sin impulsively with their lips. Angry words, like sparks, kindle fires which hurt both themselves and others. If these soon die, they still leave their mark and grieve the Spirit of the Lord. Their consequences may also be very far-reaching and unpredictable. And however much we seek to justify ourselves when we give way to anger, we are still reminded that "the wrath of man worketh not the righteousness of God." Anger or indignation, on the human level, is seldom holy.

The Bible provides us with instances of meek and holy men who fell before ill-temper and before the ungoverned tongue. There is an element of mystery about Moses' sin

when he twice smote the rock at Rephadim; but one
thing is clear — anger made him speak "unadvisedly with
his lips." Instead of ascribing the miracle of the smitten
rock to God he ascribed it to Aaron and himself. "Must
we fetch you water out of this rock?" In that hour he
came under God's just rebuke, and by that one impulsive
act and word he excluded himself from the Promised
Land. He was one of the greatest of men, and meek of
spirit. He was God's friend, dwelling daily in His presence.
But he was not outwith the reach of God's chastening
rod when sin reared its ugly head in his conduct.

It is a well-known fact that our irritations often come
with physical weariness. A sleepless night does not leave
us in the best of humour in the morning. Was there ever,
for example, a more devoted follower of his Master than
Simon Peter? In his heart there was an ever-deepening
love for his Lord. When he stood before Him "who knows
all things" he invited Him to look into his heart where
He might see that holy flame of spiritual love casting its
glow through the whole of his spirit. "Thou knowest,
Lord, that I love Thee." Yet, under the repeated irritations of that early morning, when he denied the Loved
One, he gave way to temper and unbecoming words.
Sleep, "the balm of weary minds," had fled away before
the terrors of that hour. Satan was on the prowl; it was
his opportune moment to attack a weary and frightened
follower of the Lord. He would sift him as wheat. And
when the full force of that unexpected temptation assailed
his soul he, for the moment, fell. For that sin he was
instantly forgiven, but in this world he could not forgive
himself. He never put forward any excuse for his terrible
lapse. Christ sweetened his sorrow by His forgiveness,
His love, and forgetfulness of it; but penitence remained

with him to the end. Christ restored to him "the joy of his salvation," and filled his soul again with His peace.

And as He forgives us we ought also to forgive one another. This is how Christ's spirit within us shows itself.

Many years ago, in one of our Scottish parishes, a large congregation could be seen waiting one day for the service to begin. When the minister at last appeared, instead of going to the pulpit, he walked toward the elders' pew. "Please forgive me," he said to one of his friends who sat there. When the grace of forgiveness was duly exercised and expressed between them both, the minister went up to the pulpit and preached his sermon. But his "sharp words" to a beloved friend left a shadow over his soul for many days. In contrast to this how damaging it is to the soul to nurse an ugly grudge against a fellow creature! And how often have we detected this evil among men who should be the last to harbour it. This is a sin which all who fear the Lord should strangle at its birth.

Many of us live with sad memories. An incident which still haunts my memory had to do with a man — a professing Christian — who believed that some of his friends had "turned against him." On account of this imaginary misdeed the devil ploughed a dark furrow in his soul. Now he was on his death-bed. When I sat down beside him I told him, very gently, how wrong he was in his attitude to his friends, and how — even if his complaint was well-founded — he should forgive all men as the Lord commanded. But no. In a hard volcanic voice he replied: "I will never forgive any of them." At that moment I left the room amazed that any man would venture into the presence of "the Judge of all the earth"

with such a root of bitterness in his heart. And yet I
hope my friend is now in Heaven, and that one day we
shall meet again in that blessed place where Satan shall
trouble us no more.

A man of God once preached a sermon on the subject
of Christian patience and forgiveness. This good man
had been the subject of much misrepresentation, if not
persecution. His season in the furnace of affliction was
long and unrelieved. Now he was addressing a large
gathering in one of our Scottish towns. His theme was
the disposition and long suffering of the holy children
in the Babylonian furnace. He mentioned the solemn
fact that when they emerged out of their ordeal not even
the smell of the fire clung to them. And God's people,
he reminded his audience, who sometimes suffer under
a persecuting spirit, should not display the least trace of
ill-will toward those who hurt them. Even "the smell" of
resentment must not cling to their beings. To whatever
cross they are nailed, or however hot the fire into which
they are cast, their voice and heart should echo the spirit
of Him Who said, "Father, forgive them . . . ," or of him
who prayed with his last breath, "Lord, lay not this sin
to their charge." But for this we need much patience and
the exercise of that love which suffers long and is kind.

I once sat in a church. I was just a boy at the time.
It was a Fellowship meeting at which a number of men
gave the appropriate "marks" of grace which belong to
those whose hearts are changed and who know the Lord.
It was left to a young man to end the discussion. Of all
that was said that evening I now remember nothing
except one remark by this man. "When Christ," he said,
"forgave me my sins, and when His love touched my
heart, I would, if need be, have carried on my back my

greatest enemy, even though he were a tramp."

When, therefore, provocations, like thorns, appear in our pathway, and when, as a result, we are overcome by a hasty spirit and utter hasty words, let grace take over and let patience and forgiveness continue their perfect work. And if the struggle is sore and continuous, let us take comfort from God's promise — "He will subdue our iniquities, and cast all our sins into the depth of the sea."

Sometimes as we feel anger surging through our spirit we may be tempted to question whether God's saving power has ever really changed our lives. Where are the meekness and gentleness of Christ which we ought to exhibit? Where is the image of our Lord which we profess to bear?

Some may have heard the story of a good man who was once on his way to church. A great grief racked his mind. Tears of sorrow filled his eyes. His easily-ruffled temper was his persistent cross. Through the sudden clouds which so often descended on his spirit he could not detect the jewel of grace. That day, as he sat in church, the minister used an illustration. He spoke about the ark of God in the wilderness, and now it was covered with the skins of rams and of goats. The gold was there hidden and unseen beneath the unattractive coverings. And in the same way, added the preacher, a gracious soul may lie beneath the rough externals of temperamental infirmities. Only when our pilgrimage is over shall these be removed and we appear in the perfect likeness of Him Who loved us. In the nature of things our temperamental lapses often happen in the presence of our fellow men; but there are other evils more destructive of our spiritual well-being than any mere flash of unguarded temper. These work their way inward into our deeper selves, and apart from casual revelations are seldom seen of men. Sometimes the mask comes off and the other, hidden, man of the heart appears in the form of some deep besetting sin.

Many of the Lord's people, for example, struggle against the sin of pride, the sin of covetousness, or the sin of unchaste thought or imagination. "Mr Self" — as the older generation used to designate the evil of pride — likes to sit on a throne. He ever strives for the first place. Unlike the Lord on earth, he is never clothed in humility, and ignores God's terrible warning with regard to the coming day when all human categories shall be reversed, and when "the first shall be last and the last first." It takes great grace to subdue this tendency of our fallen nature, and to say — "He must increase, but I must decrease." Our sorest struggle, on the other hand, may be with unchaste thoughts. This is a "plague of the heart," or a "giant lust," that has brought many into the vale of grief. In an age when this sin is looked upon by many as a legitimate expression of our instinctive life, it behoves all who love the Lord to make a covenant with both their ears and their eyes. And have we not known those who must be constantly on their guard against some of the habits of their unregenerate days? Although in many cases these habits are for ever slain in the day of God's power, there are others whose struggle against "the past" is both terrible and real.

There are many other sins which strive against the gracious soul, but whatever their nature we must never confront them in our own strength. When Simon Peter listened to his Lord as He spoke of His being left alone in the hour of His agony, he could not conceive of himself as falling so low. "Though all men shall be offended because of Thee, yet will I never be offended." This was the voice of a self-confident man, who, as yet, knew only a little of sin's power or of Satan's wiles, and who would venture into any situation in his own strength. But he was the first to fall when the awful blast from hell was let loose on him and his companions. No; our strength is never in ourselves. "Without Me, ye can do nothing." But, I can do all things through Christ who strengtheneth me."

David faced the giant in the name of the Lord. Because he had put on the whole armour of God he refused Saul's armour. The one excludes the other. To worldly eyes he was very foolish; but as he stepped into the fray he knew that, trusting in God, victory was his. From the running brook he took five smooth stones, and in a moment one of these lay deeply buried in the giant's skull. When the enemy of our soul, therefore, seeks to hurt and ensnare us through our besetting sin, let us kneel by the brook of Truth and trust in His Word. One promise flung in the devil's face is enough to bring him low. "It is written . . ." Faith in God, and in His promise to help us in the hour of danger, is the soul's ultimate way of escape. "Almost," said David, "they had consumed me on the earth." What a word is this! "Almost," — but not altogether! What volumes could each child of God write around that one word? What miracles of deliverance and preservation lie within its bosom! What tokens of the love of God and of His unfailing care nestle at its heart! How often, through our besetting sins, have our feet touched the brink of moral or spiritual destruction! And only for the strong preventive Hand of Him who keeps His Israel in every age we would have gone over.

> Unless the Lord had been my help
>> When I was sore opprest
> Almost my soul had in the house
>> Of silence been at rest.
> When I had uttered this word,
>> My foot doth slip away,
> Thy mercy held me up, O Lord,
>> Thy goodness did me stay.

When we mourn, because by our besetting sins we so often grieve the Holy Spirit and alienate the conscious presence of the Lord from our souls, we cannot at the same time but wonder at His forebearancce and mercy. To all such how precious are the words: "Who is a God like unto thee, that pardoneth iniquity, and passeth by the transgression of the remnant of thine heritage? He retaineth not His anger for ever, because he delighteth in mercy. He will turn again, he will have compassion upon us; he will subdue our iniquities; and thou wilt cast all their sins into the depths of the sea."

CHAPTER V.

THE FEARS OF THE FLOCK

FEAR entered our world, and took possession of man's heart, when he fell away from God. After his great transgression we find Adam trying to hide himself from God "among the trees of the garden." There he stood shivering in his guilt, and already deeply conscious of the perils to which his sin had exposed him. "I was afraid," were the first dread words which fell from his lips. We see him with his back to his Maker, and He in Whose perfect fellowship fear was unknown. now departed from him. And because Adam was the root of mankind, and the federal head of the race, we must necessarily share in his woe. Fear is, therefore, something which lies in the bosom of all men; and all are involved in his guilt. The grace of God in the heart of His people is no guarantee that fear is for ever removed. "Fear not," is, indeed, an endearing word from the lips of our Lord; but it also implies that fear in some form is ever present with us. When we look into our Bible we find that many of those who had God as their Friend in this world were often overtaken by fear. Situations emerged in their world and in their personal lives which often filled them with concern.

In this chapter, however, we are not concerned with "natural," instinctive, or even sinful fear, or with those recognised sources of anxiety which belong to this age.

These sources of fear in the modern world we hope to mention later. At this point we would refer to the causes of those spiritual anxieties which secretly lodge in the bosom of some of God's people. These are fears, we believe, which are peculiar to a genuine Christian experience, and to those who understand something of the dangers and deceptions which ensnare many in our own day.

Who, for example, can read the parable of the Ten Virgins without a measure of real concern? The foolish ones, apparently, never doubted their own good standing with the Heavenly Bridegroom for Whom, in their own way, they looked and for Whom they waited. They never doubted that they would receive a kindly welcome at His door. They never envisaged the dread crisis of the midnight hour, or the death of their hope in the corridor of death. The thought never crossed their mind that He would fail to recognise their voice when they would stand at His door. The parable is solemn in that it teaches that many of those who make a profession of God within the visible Church are strangers to God. The wholesome spiritual concern of the true Christian is, therefore, not to be despised. It is, indeed, a good anchor to preserve us from the treacherous rocks of presumption and spiritual pride.

Not long ago a man wrote me a letter. In it he expressed his concern over his own spiritual condition. Some of his friends claimed that they had received "the fulness of the Spirit," or what they called "the second blessing." This had brought them to the coveted heights of "total consecration" and the living of a "victorious" Christian life. They had emerged out of their spiritual poverty, weakness and perplexities. This man wanted to know if their claims were Scriptural and consistent with true Christian experience.

While some may envy those who make such claims — and we cannot question the sincerity of those who make them — the ideal picture of the true believer, or the truly blessed, is given by our Lord Himself in His Word. Where does He begin? "Blessed are the poor in spirit; for theirs is the Kingdom of Heaven. Blessed are they that mourn: for they shall be comforted. Blessed are they who do hunger and thirst after righteousness: for they shall be filled." "To this man will I look, even to him that is poor and of a contrite spirit and trembleth at my word."

It is by the door of our ever growing sense of humility, sin and need that we enter the Kingdom of Heaven — not only the kingdom of grace, but of glory as well.

It is in the Valley of Humiliation that we fear no fall. **Mr Fearing, Mr Poor Man** and **Miss Much-Afraid** are, indeed, familiar types in Christ's fold.

But here let me mention some of the sources from which the fear of many of God's people arise. There are those, for example, who are often distressed with anxieties which have to do with their standing before God. We have known many such.

Some are afraid that the beginnings of their Christian life are unsound, and that their lamps also may go out at the midnight hour. Since they cannot name the means by which God at first awakened them out of death's slumber, or point to the hour when they passed from death to life, they fear their hope is false. They know little or nothing of the vivid and shattering events which accompanied the conversion of men like Paul, John Newton, the Phillipian Jailer, and many others besides.

Their hope was born with the still small voice of God's Spirit within their hearts, or with a gentle resting of their affections on Christ. As with Lydia, the Lord by a mere touch of His love and power opened their hearts.

God, however, is as effectually present in the dew of His grace as He is in the stroke of His sword or in the thunder of His power.

In comforting some of the Lord's people Charles H. Spurgeon used to say that "we need not know the day of our birth to prove that we live." Is not our life here a proof that we were born? And our spiritual needs and desires prove that we are born again. Spiritual existence presupposes spiritual birth. The desire of the new-born babe is one evidence of its new life in Christ.

Once I met an elderly lady who, throughout the years, showed how greatly she valued and loved the means of grace and the Word of God. But although true faith lodged in her heart she was all her life under a cloud of concern with regard to her interest in Christ. She was only eleven years old when she listened to an earnest minister of Christ preaching from the words: "Whither shall I go from thy Spirit?" (Psalm 139). That sermon made a lasting impression on her. But she was only a girl at the time and easily touched in her emotions! Could it be that the impression of her childhood days was truly of God? This was the persistent question which occupied her mind. When I spoke of her long years of love and devotion to the Lord and His cause as solid proofs of a saving change in her life, the cloud of fear which had so long cast its shadow over her soul began to lift. The following day she sat for the first time at the Lord's Table — assured that the Lord was the portion of her soul.

In one of my congregations we had a choice young man whose life bore the stamp of godliness, but who, for a similar reason, stood aloof from making a public profession of his faith. "God's people have something which I lack," was the sad word which was often on his lips. They were, he thought, more sure of their beginnings in the life of grace, and enjoyed a greater assurance of their election in Christ, and of His everlasting love, than he. While he loved their company he was afraid he was not one of their number. The day came, however, when he was enabled, to say from his heart, "Thy people shall be my people and thy God my God." He discovered that his spiritual sympathies and affinities were with those who follow the Lamb, and that they were no strangers to the fears which distressed his own soul.

Many tender souls move under such shadows all their days. There is a fear in their heart both with regard to their effectual calling by the Holy Spirit, and their election in Christ. The two go together, and for that reason we are exhorted to make both "sure." How, they ask, may we know that God's love rested on us from all eternity and that our names are in the Lamb's book of life?

For the encouragement of those who are cast down because they lack this full assurance, I should like to relate the following story. In the North of Scotland a large congregation once sat listening to approved men of God who testified to their interest in Christ. The "Question" was based on this same exhortation, "to make our calling and election sure." To some this theme was a great deep. There was present an old soldier, however, who, when he was asked to make his comment on this subject, brought honey and sweetness out of the words. As a pensioned soldier, the King's allowance came into his hand with unfailing regularity. He had never seen his name in "the big book in London," but the King's money, which he carried in his purse, was the evidence that his name was truly there. In the same way God's people get their daily portion of grace from the Lord's hand, and this is the proof that their names are written in the Book of life. The Lord refreshes them with "a drink from the well of Bethlehem which is by the gate." This is "the earnest" of their eternal enjoyment of the pleasures which are for ever more at His right hand. They sit lowly at His feet where sweet "crumbs" of His love and grace reach their waiting souls. This is the proof that God is preparing a table for them where "they shall hunger no more neither thirst any more." One drop of the love of Christ in our heart and one promise applied to our mind by the Holy Spirit, are, indeed, the earnest that we are to enjoy and inherit these, in all their fulness, by and by.

In that large congregation there were not a few to whom such words were a cup of consolation.

Are there not others who once believed that they had such an assurance of God's love, but who fear that, with a persistent and prolonged coldness creeping over their affections, their early assurance had no roots in reality? With David they say:

> "How long wilt thou forget me, Lord,
>   Shall it for ever be?
> O, how long shall it be that thou
>   Wilt hide Thy face from me?"

William Cowper expressed in memorable words the holy concern which often lies in the bosom of God's people.

"Where is the blessedness I knew
    When first I saw the Lord?
Where is the soul-refreshing view
    Of Jesus and His Word?
What peaceful hours I once enjoyed
    How sweet their memory still!
But they have left an aching void
    The world can never fill."

But is not this anxiety in itself a real proof that we still possess what we fear to have lost? The famous Hector MacPhail of Resolis once spoke about the cry of Job: "O that I knew where I might find Him." "Where," he asked, "shall we find Christ for Job? May we not find Him within that cry and desire in his own heart?"

A company of Christian people met one day in a certain home. Among them was a young woman whose heart the Lord had savingly touched. But at that moment she was full of grief, for she feared that her earlier love to her Lord had died in her heart. Then the door opened and in walked a tall, elderly man who was a total stranger to her. As he stood before the company he said, "Who among you loves the Lord most? . . . . You, poor soul," he said, "who are full of fear that your love to Him has died in your heart." Then he went on his way, but to her he was a messenger of God. Instantly her hope revived and her heart began to burn within her. Christ was in her heart in spite of all her fears.

One of my treasured memories is a conversation I once had with an old man in a Glasgow hospital. In his earlier days this man enjoyed great nearness to the Lord; but his time of favour had seemed to come to an end. For many years he walked without the light of the Sun and afraid that he was deceived in his hope. But as he spoke one could see that he was now enjoying "the latter rain" of the Lord's renewing grace. The Lord, he told us, had restored to him the joy of his salvation. Thus, as it often happens, our spiritual anxieties are frequently in themselves an evidence of our regeneration. This sense of desertion is something of which "Talkatives" and "Formalists" know nothing. A dead formalism is always satisfied with its own pretty shroud. Jerusalem's daughters never cried out, "Saw ye Him whom my soul loveth?" This, however, is often the cry of the Bride here.

This spiritual concern was well illustrated by a comment made by an eminent Christian man — Duncan MacRae of Lochalsh — who once gave his Christian witness at a public meeting. He told a story of his boyhood days when a wealthy stranger met him in the way and gave him a silver coin. When he placed the welcome coin in his pocket he felt he was the richest person in the land! Then he went on his way rejoicing. But when he had walked a while in the way he put his hand in his pocket to discover that he had lost his treasure. His joy was turned into sorrow. In this downcast state he walked on in the path which lay through the heath. As his fingers moved in his empty pocket he found in the corner the hole through which the coin had slipped. Then to his great astonishment and joy he discovered that the coin lay safely in the lower lining of his jacket! "If," said Duncan, "my first joy was great, my joy in finding what I had thought to have lost was greater still." Duncan found in this incident an example of the way in which God's people may sometimes mourn over the seeming loss of what they can never lose — the life and the love of God in their souls. His love is there for ever, though its assurance may at times be absent. That love is shed abroad in their hearts by the Holy Spirit who is to abide with them for ever.

It appears that one of Mr Fearing's greatest anxieties was concerned with his final acceptance at God's door. What if these words addressed to the foolish virgins would seal his eternal rejection also? "I never knew you." A preacher once mentioned these words in a sermon. Then he asked a question: "What did the Lord mean when He addressed these words to the foolish virgins? Did He not mean that, for one thing, their voice was strange to Him? He had never heard them truly at the Throne of Grace. Their hearts, affections and desires were far removed from His on earth. Their voice was not that of His children whose prayers on earth reached His ear out of a contrite heart and a broken spirit. The Lord would never have said this of any of His own. As they know His voice He knows theirs. He knows the voice of his dove, and the cry of the poor and the needy. They can say as He speaks to them out of His Word 'The voice of my Beloved.' And to those who take refuge under His wings He says 'Let Me hear thy voice.' Dear people of God, are you afraid your voice which, sometimes weeping on His bosom, He has so often heard on earth, He will not know when you come to His door? Comfort your heart for that cannot happen." Is this saying not a well of comfort to those "who mourn after a godly sort?"

Perhaps, however, some of our greatest fears come through the sterner and darker processes of God's holy Providence. We sometimes fear that these, instead of being tokens of His love, are the earnests of His wrath. Job was a man greatly loved of God, but when the mysterious wheel of Providence took an adverse turn he cried in anguish, "the terrors of God do set themselves in array against me." There is really no conflict between God's promise and God's providence. God assures us in His Word that all things work together for our good; but often, like Jacob, bowed down in grief, we say, "All these things are against me." We only see our own side of the hill. But the God Who sees it all reassures us that all is well. His bow is for ever in the cloud, the sign of His covenant, faithfulness and love.

In the lovely parish of Gairloch in Ross-shire, a woman once sat in a large congregation listening to a sermon. The preacher spoke of the fears which often arise in the bosom of God's people over this apparent conflict between God's promise and God's Providence. Part of the sermon was based on the story of Abraham at Mount Moriah. At the last moment God arrested the weapon with which, at God's own command, he was to slay his well-beloved son of promise. "If," the preacher said, "God gave you His promise, the day may come when, in the trial of your faith, the sharp knife of His Providence may come within an inch of its life; but be sure of this — the promise shall never be slain."

The excellent Mrs Vitch, whose story of God's faithfulness is one of the gems of Covenanting literature, often stood trembling under trials which seemed, at the time, to undo the promises which God had sealed on her heart as she wrestled with Him in prayer. In the evening of her days, however, as she looked back on the way in which God had led her she wrote the words: "Now I know that His promises shall neither die nor drown."

CHAPTER VI.

THE GREAT ADVERSARY

THE BIBLE, as a supernatural Revelation, speaks everywhere of a destructive spiritual power or being who is active in every area of life. This satanic person is spoken of under many significant and awe-inspiring names. His great aim is to impede God in all His purposes and, if that were possible, to destroy all who are on His side. The origin of evil is, needless to say, a deep mystery; but that such a power is present in our world should be obvious to all. The whole world, according to Scripture, is lying under his sway.

Spiritual wickedness, or Satan, is not, as the Bible reveals, a blind, mindless power without purpose or plan of his own. He is a person, if also only a creature. He is highly intelligent, and, in his own terrible way, unified in all his aims. The devil, and all who follow in his wake, are not, as our Lord warned us, a divided house, but a well-organised army. These fight continually for the soul of man, and for his ultimate involvement in their own punishment. Their sphere of operation is not confined to the circumference of life. They make man's soul their abode. They are at work within the visible Church, and through the various "religions" and "cults" which emerge in the world. Satan has often transformed himself into an angel of light. Man is the willing tool through which he defiles the world, and deceives the millions who think that their "religion" is of God. Through fallen man —

who has become his slave — he perpetuates the process
of degeneration, lawlessness and confusion which the
pages of history present to the eye. And in our blindness
we ascribe these things to other causes and trace them to
other sources. Many are unaware of Satan's presence.
Many deny his existence. As the arch-deceiver he is able
to conceal himself while we may be dominated by his
will. And this is how he wants us to remain.

The newly-born Christians at Ephesus, whom Paul
warned against "spiritual wickedness," had once been
dead to God and dead in sin. So much so that any
warning such as reached them in their converted state
would have then fallen on unbelieving ears. But now
awakened out of their spiritual sleep, and in the ranks
of the Just, they knew something of the depths and wiles
of Satan. Only the true Church of God has this awareness of Satan's presence and power in the world. It is
one evidence of her spiritual change and of her love to
God. Because the Church of Christ bears the treasure of
Truth, and because Christ dwells in her heart by faith,
Satan will pursue her to the end. She is the enemy of
sin; and in her warfare against evil she is "terrible as an
army with banners."

The figures which are used in the Bible to describe
Satan should put us on our guard. In his strength he is
the "roaring lion which goeth about seeking whom he
may devour." In his deception he is the old serpent whose
fangs are steeped in lies. He is the arch-slanderer, or the
accuser of the brethren. That is what the word "devil"
means. He is apolyon, or the destroyer. He is "the great
red dragon" who keeps the nations of this world in a
state of agitation. He never sleeps, and for that reason
we should always watch and pray. He moves to and fro

on the earth, and wherever he sees God's image imprinted on any life he will seek to erase it. If his power is limited, we should not for that reason minimise it. Only that God sets restraining bounds to his wrath we would easily become his prey. If the image of God is imprinted on our life and conduct his malice toward us shall know no bounds.

A dread example of Satan's hatred of the saints is seen in the life of Job. This holy man lived in daily communion with God, and walked in the light of His face. He had no spiritual counterpart in his age. And God permitted that he should be cast into a furnace of affliction, and sifted in Satan's sieve. Like Joseph, Daniel and Paul he suffered not for his sins but for his holiness of life. Satan's insinuation was that if God took away his earthly prosperity, and afflicted his life with pain, he would curse him to His face. Apparently Job was unaware that the adversary had any hand in his woes. He speaks of "the terrors of God" as putting themselves in array against him. Satan was in the background, but concealed. But he could not move a finger except as the Lord allowed. The Devil is tethered by God's will, and the arm which restrains him is omnipotent.

In such seasons of conflict the questions which shaped themselves in Job's mind may be present with us also when we are brought into similar trials. What has happened? we ask. How could it happen? And why? The loving God of yesterday hides Himself behind a thick cloud of adversity. The fair world of our dreams collapses. A load of depression lies on our mind. Satan's fiery darts pierce through our soul. In these sudden and unexpected trials we often fail to see God's wisdom in allowing Satan to buffet us. The Bible everywhere warns

us against any illusions of going to heaven without conflict. This was, at times, Job's fond but untried hope.
"I shall die in my nest." "Beloved, think it not strange,
concerning the fiery trial which is to try you, as though
some strange thing happened unto you . . . . Be sober,
be vigilant because your adversary the Devil, as a roaring
lion, walketh about seeking whom he may devour: whom
resist steadfast in the faith, knowing that the same
afflictions are accomplished in your brethren that are in
the world" (I. Peter, 5).

There are trials which, because of their sheer dread,
we lock up in our own breasts, and hide from all except
from Him Who is our unfailing Friend and Deliverer.
When, for example, Job was in the depths of affliction he
reasoned that "strangling" was preferable to life. The
same temptation threw its toils over the spirit of Christian
as he lay low in Doubting Castle. The gracious William
Cowper had to contend with a similar temptation over a
long period of his Christian life; but God was His Shield
to the end. The adversary may also come — as he came
to our blessed Lord when he desired Him to worship him
— as a spirit of blasphemy, thereby sinking the mind in a
great fear. But the fact that such thoughts are repugnant
to our mind, grievous to our heart, and that we would
give a million worlds to be rid of them for ever, prove
that Satan is their instigator.

Men like John Bunyan and "Fraser of Brae," have dis-
closed a little of the terrors with which Satan assailed their
spirits; but the great majority of those who have passed
through those dark vales, would never relate what they
had to endure in this way. Thomas Guthrie remarks
that such distressing thoughts and fears — such as we
have mentioned — are present with many of the saints,

and that those who do commit an unpardonable sin against the Holy Spirit are wholly free from these fears. Their minds are darkened. Their conscience is seared. Their hearts are full of enmity against God. It is the sin of those who hate Christ; who, consciously and deliberately, reject the witness of the Holy Spirit concerning Him in the Written Word. They are men who are fixed in their resentment against Christ. The point which one would stress here is that, in itself, temptation, however violent, ugly, and distracting it may appear, is no sin. Only when by a deliberate act of the will we yield to it does it become a sin. While in all its terror it may invade the mind and the imagination, if we still resist it, and hate its voice and suggestions, no sin is involved. Satan may come in like a flood, and our own corrupt nature may erupt in a way that may fill us with fear, but if we endure or resist it we are, before God, counted as blessed. "Blessed is the man that endureth temptation: for when he is tried he shall receive the crown of life which the Lord hath promised to them that love him."

When C. H. Spurgeon was once severely tortured by evil thoughts he asked his grandfather if such thoughts did not prove that he was no true Christian. "Nonsense, Charles," replied the old man, "these blasphemies are no children of yours. They are the devil's brats which he delights to leave at the door of a Christian. Do not own them as yours. Give them neither house-room nor heart-room."

Instances could be given of men and women who lived very near the Lord, but whom Satan pursued in this way over long seasons. There was, to give one example, an eminent and holy minister of Christ in the North of Scotland who, because of the flood of evil thoughts which sometimes passed over his soul, was afraid to sleep for fear that he might awake in a lost eternity. But the God of peace bruised Satan under his feet, and his soul was at last wafted into Heaven on a wave of joy. Another man used to smite his own mouth lest his lips would give voice to the dark thoughts which irresistably invaded his soul. But in his case, also, the Lord made him listen to His Word as He pronounced him righteous, forgiven, and an heir of eternal salvation, through His well-beloved Son.

Let me at this point give a more extended account of a soul in distress because, I believe, the story is typical of the sufferings and fears of many of God's people. The elect lady who wrote this account of her own anguish of soul was Mrs E. Banfield from England.

"About this time," she wrote, "awful and blasphemous thoughts rushed into my mind against the Lord, that I had no control over. I felt there could be no pardon for me now. I could neither sleep nor eat, or attend to the affairs of this life; but sank into an anguish and agony of mind which words cannot express. One day venturing to look into the Bible, I opened upon these words, 'Whosoever speaketh against the Holy Ghost, it shall not be forgiven him, neither in his world, neither in the world to come' (Matt. xii. 32). This quite cut me down; it was the word of God, and I believed it. My anguish of mind was indeed great; I feared day by day that I should not be suffered to open my eyes again in the land of the living, and felt my case was so bad that I must not presume even to ask for mercy. I felt I was lost, and could truly say, 'The pains of hell gat hold upon me; I found trouble and sorrow.'

"I can remember walking my room at this time under

a most dreadful temptation to take my life. O what earnest cries this caused that I might die a natural death, though I had not the least hope, and believed that everlasting misery would be my portion hereafter!

"Soon after, taking up Bunyan's 'Pilgrim's Progress,' I opened upon where Christian is made to believe he spake blasphemies, when it was Satan injecting them into his mind. This seemed to throw a ray of light across my path, and with it, a 'who can tell?' sprang up within, 'but that I may find mercy yet.' I kept going to that book to read it over again and again, and it created fresh cries in my heart for deliverance. In this way I went on for some time, with now and then a gleam of hope, which would soon vanish; when in agony of mind I would wish I had never been born, or like the beast possessed no soul which must live for ever.

"One morning I went to my room overwhelmed with grief, and I cried, 'Lord, Thou must come, for I cannot bear it any longer. It is mercy I want'; when to the eye of faith, I had such a view of Christ dying upon the cross. And one portion of Scripture after another came rolling into my mind with such sweetness and power: 'As Moses lifted up the serpent in the wilderness, even so must the Son of Man be lifted up, that whosoever believeth in Him should not perish, but have everlasting life'; and 'Come unto Me, all ye that labour and are heavy laden, and I will give you rest.' As one word after another was applied, such light and understanding accompanied them, and in simplicity I wondered how it was I had not seen before what I then saw. I was now brought to that sweet and sacred spot, to weep at the dear feet of my blessed Redeemer; and I cried, 'If I perish, I must perish here, looking unto Jesus.' I was like one taken from Mount Sinai and brought to Calvary, and inexpressible love flowed into my heart. I said, 'Lord, I do believe, and Thou art able to save me.' I cannot find words to describe the change. The dark cloud which had so long hung over me was gone; Satan and his accusations had fled, and in their place peace which passeth all understanding flowed into my soul. How differently I laid my head upon the pillow that night! 'I looked for hell, he brought me heaven.' What happiness is to be compared to a taste of Christ's love? The fear of death and hell was removed, for I had found a resting-place in that dear wounded side."

What infinite consolation may we derive from the promise that, in Christ, God has forgiven, covered and forgotten all the sins of His people! They are for ever put away "as far as the east is distant from the west." They are remembered no more. None of their sins can ever rise beyond the infinite merits of their infinite and loving Redeemer. An old English minister spoke on his death-bed of the comfort he derived from what he called God's **"act of oblivion"** within the provisions and the promises of that covenant which is ordered in all things and sure. "Thy sins and thine iniquities I will remember no more." They are for ever "blotted out as a thick cloud."

Let those, therefore, of God's children who are afraid that these floods out of Satan's mouth have brought them under God's eternal displeasure, be assured that there are thousands singing before the Throne in glory who had been through the same great tribulation here. The day will come when these dark waters shall subside, and when their sun shall arise to go down no more. "For this is as the waters of Noah unto me: for as I have sworn that the waters of Noah should no more go over the earth; so have I sworn that I would not be wroth with thee, nor rebuke thee. For the mountains shall depart and the hills be removed; but my kindness shall not depart from thee, neither shall the covenant of my peace be removed, saith the Lord that hath mercy on thee."

In his assaults on the people of God there is not in Satan's armoury a more dangerous weapon than that of unbelief. This was the sin by which he brought all mankind so low. "Hath God said?" This was hell's lie in the form of a question mark. In the catalogue of human woe no sin is more destructive than this. It is a sin which contradicts the One who cannot lie. Those who are in a state of grace know that this sin is not overcome in a day. We seek to crucify it, but it refuses to die.

God, for example, gives His people His word of promise. And, in the words of John Bunyan, it may come into our soul bearing the flavour of heaven and bathed in the love of Christ. When the promise is given in such a context of consolation we rest in the absolute and eternal trustworthiness of Him who gave it.

Then we come to some Slough of Despond when unbelief takes possession of our mind. Satan will do all in his power to extinguish our hope and drown our comforts in unbelief. Many of God's choice saints have often lived over long periods of time with the dark shadow of Doubt over their spirits.

I once listened to an outstanding preacher who told his audience of an eminent man of God who, in the grasp of unbelieving fears, cried: "O God! if there be a God, save my soul, if I have a soul!" If in such storms, when like Peter, we begin to sink, we should remember that hell never forged a weapon that can make the promise of God to His people of none effect.

One evening, many years ago, a strange compulsive feeling held my mind. It was that someone in my congregation was in distress and needed "a word in season." A few minutes afterwards I was led to knock at a certain door where I was welcomed by a woman whose sorrow of heart showed in her very eyes. She spoke sadly about the great fear which banished sleep from her eyes the previous night — apart from a brief hour about the dawn of day. "If only," she remarked, "I could lay hold on the words with which I awoke out of that needed hour of rest how happy I would be!" When I asked her what this word was, she quoted, as I remember, the words of Psalm Thirty-seven:

> "Delight thyself in God; He'll give
> Thine heart's desire to thee.
> Thy way to God commit, Him trust,
> It bring to pass shall He."

"These words," I said, "were from God to your soul. And let me tell you that your spiritual safety here, and your everlasting happiness with God in the world to come, are embraced in that word." There and then I left her to drink her cup of joy. Her faith revived, and the enemy who had harassed her for many days moved away. He knew that she now carried a sword in her hand with which she could vanquish him.

If there are temptations which fill us with fear there are others that we easily endure. The apostle Paul, in writing to the Thessalonians, speaks about his having been hindered by Satan in the Lord's work. All, indeed, who would live a useful Christian life know something of

Satan's power to hinder them in the path of duty. One of his favourite tactics is that of diverting our mind from our more important spiritual activities to the more trivial concerns of our daily life. Sometimes, for example, we find ourselves with time on our hands — a precious gift which God exhorts us to redeem. The wholesome thought may then come into our mind that we should go aside to pray. But another and a contrary thought rushes in upon us! "I really ought to pray, but at the moment I must relax for a while. There are a few things which demand my attention. And, who knows, but my friends may call . . ." It is at this point that Satan — if he is capable of such an act — laughs over his easy victory. The prayer of God's people is what he dreads; for the weapon of all prayer has often brought him low in many of his designs!

Even when we do go aside to pray he may follow us and make short work of our devotions. "That's enough. You have too much to do! What about that letter you were to write? And you have forgotten . . . ." We then walk away to discover that these suggestions have all lost their urgency!

The Devil may also appear on the scene as our accuser. He can discourage us by pointing to the inconsistencies and the blemishes which so often mar our life. When Joshua, the high priest, stood before God in his soiled garments the devil stood by with his mouth full of mockings and accusations. God's saint was silent, and so was the attendant angel. But not his great Advocate in heaven. "And the Lord said unto Satan, the Lord rebuke thee, O Satan; even the Lord who hath chosen Jerusalem rebuke thee. Is not this a brand plucked out of the fire?" (Zech. 3). To argue with Satan is futile.

We can only lift up our eyes and our voice to Him Who
is our strong Tower and Shield. It was the excellent
Catherine Bretterege who once, after a great conflict
with Satan, said "Reason not with me, I am but a weak
woman; if thou hast anything to say, say it to my Christ.
He is my Advocate, my strength and my Redeemer, and
He shall plead my cause."

Satan sometimes tries to ensnare us through our
instincts and through the motions of the flesh which
war against the spirit. We read of Job that he had
made "a covenant with his eyes." But many have fallen
where he had stood. By this sin David remained for
many days in the depths of grief. On the other hand,
the grace of God in its preserving power is nowhere seen
more impressively than in the life of Joseph. With that
grace went a tenderness of conscience, a watchful spirit,
and a constant awareness that God's eye was ever upon
him. He was aware of the peril to which he was exposed
in a land where the true fear of God was unknown. Day
after day the soft enticing voice of an adulterous woman
sounded in his ear. "We have the house all to ourselves;
come lie down beside me." He knew also what the
result of his refusal would be. But a conscience void of
offence was a greater treasure by far than mere social
security, or the precarious pleasures of sin. The unclean
act he speaks of as "a great wickedness," and "a sin
against God." In Joseph's conflict with Satan God's
grace won the day.

We mentioned that the word "devil" means "a slan-
derer." He would have his revenge on Joseph by filling
the mouth of this woman with lies. She would mis-
represent him to her "lord," and to the whole community,
as a degenerate slave who had tried to humiliate her in

her own home. And, as it often happens, the lie was believed; and for many days he lived under the shadow of scandal. "But the Lord was with Joseph."

During the Great Evangelical Revival there were several eminent preachers in England and Scotland who had made heavy breaches on the kingdom of Satan. And Satan tried to arrest their work by throwing this very shadow over their name. The trial, in each case, was so unexpected, and so full of terror, that only for God's sustaining grace they would have broken under its weight. One good man would writhe in agony on the floor of his room wondering how such a lie could be born. Another left for a distant land till God, by His word, arrested his footsteps and commanded him to return to his sphere of labour. A younger man, whose labours the Lord had owned, was waylaid by a Jezebel who wanted to blot out his good name. But in each case God vindicated their names, and caused their righteousness to shine forth as the noon day. When John Bunyan was falsely accused by his enemies of unbecoming associations he could say that no woman in heaven, in hell or on earth could lay anything to his charge. How comforting are Christ's Words to all who suffer for righteousness' sake. "Blessed are ye, when men shall revile you, and shall say all manner of evil against you falsely, for My Name's sake. Rejoice and be exceeding glad, for great is your reward in heaven; for so persecuted they the prophets which were before you." Let all who trust in God rejoice in His promise. "Thanks be unto God who giveth us the victory through Jesus Christ our Lord."

During my student days I once entered a large hall in Glasgow as the minister was about to finish his sermon. As I was opening the door I could hear the impressive voice of the preacher as he addressed a large congregation. "Child of God, you have discovered that if you can put the devil once on his back, he can put you seven times on your back, but . . . . " Then followed words of comfort and reassurance for those whose trust is in the One in Whom there is "everlasting strength" and who had promised them the victory over their great foe. Around the preacher sat a goodly company of elderly Christian men who gave quiet signs that the words of the preacher had deeply touched their heart.

In those days there was another preacher in Glasgow who once illustrated the final victory of our Lord over all His and our enemies. In that victory His own people would also participate. He spoke about strong men who fought each other, and how, as it sometimes happened, the victor might, for the moment, lie on his back before he delivered the last devastating blow. Christ lay in the grave as if Death had conquered Him. To all appearances He had lost the day; but He arose again to give Death, the grave, and all the forces of darkness, the fell blow from which they would never recover. The same victory shall be given to the saints. "Because I overcame, ye also shall overcome." The day shall come in the life of every believer, when Satan and all who destroy them, shall hear their shout of victory. "Rejoice not against Me, O mine enemy: when I fall I shall arise; when I sit in darkness the Lord shall be a light unto me." (Micah 7). Their sword, and the whole armour of God, with which they fought every foe, they shall then exchange for the palm — the symbol of victory and everlasting peace. But their crown of victory they would place on the brow of Him who loved them and Who, through His own grace, made them more than conquerors.

We do not know what depths were present in those temptations with which "the son of mischief" assailed the soul of the sinless Son of God. "The prince of this world cometh and hath nothing in me." Although as the unchangeable and eternal Son of God He was incapable of sinning, yet in our nature, and as our gracious Mediator, He was tempted in all points like as we are. And because He vanquished hell on behalf of His own, none shall perish who trust in Him. The blessing of Benjamin belongs to all who look to Him for the safe keeping of their souls. "The beloved of the Lord shall dwell in safety by Him, and the Lord shall cover him all the day long, and he shall dwell between His shoulders." "When the enemy shall come in like a flood the spirit of the Lord shall lift up a standard against him."

Under His shadow we are safe.

> "Yea, in the shadow of thy wings
> My refuge I will place,
> Until these sad calamities
> Do wholly overpass.
>
> From heav'n he shall send down, and me
> From his reproach defend
> That would devour me: God His truth
> And mercy forth shall send."

CHAPTER VII

"GIANT DESPAIR"

WITH all its progress along certain lines, our age is one of increasing tensions and strain. The speed at which life is lived seems to be gathering momentum every day. The times are rushing on, and to fit into the pattern of things, we are supposed to move with them. Few care to ask as to where "the times" are moving, and most people, whether they will or no, are caught up in this ever growing restlessness. Some there are who stand up to the stresses of life more than others. Many, on the other hand, break down through sheer nervous exhaustion. This is, in fact, the age of "nervous break-downs." Unconsciously we build up tensions which result in an illness. We may reach a point where we find ourselves in a state of depression and in the grip of strange fears. Christian people suffer as acutely as others through the conflicts of life. They cannot hope to escape their own share of life's woes. This, however, does not mean that their faith in the Lord has "let them down," or that in every trial His grace is not sufficient for them. No, indeed. It just means that surrounded as they are by influences which are hostile to their spiritual life, and living in a world which, as the Lord predicted, seeks to crush them, they often fall a prey to deep depression. There are, needless to say, many other factors — often domestic and personal — which induce this condition. Some of its underlying causes may, indeed, be unknown even to themselves.

Those who, like John Bunyan in the grip of "Giant Despair," have passed through these periods of stress could speak of the dark folds of sorrow which lay over their spirits.

Let me give one example of this. It has to do with two Christian men who once travelled together. Both had been in depths of spiritual depression. The one recalled a day when, sitting in a garden, he saw a tiny creature crawling into a hole in the wall. How he envied its dim, irrational existence which, he knew, would soon end! It knew nothing of the troubles which often break in upon the spirit of man! The other mentioned an hour in his life when looking through a window in his home he saw a godless man passing by. How free and easy he was! He was ignorant of those bitter waters which are often wrung into the cup of God's child. At that moment, and like another, he was "envious at the foolish." To those who have not been in those dark vales such an attitude may seem unwise, and probably it was; but his words were expressive of the sorrow which rent his spirit for many days.

I know that what I am saying about this phase in the lives of some of God's people cannot be understood or accepted by all. Some, indeed, would dismiss it as a settled form of unbelief within our souls. It is easy to say that with almighty grace available, with all the promises of God at hand to help us, and with His own great assurance that He will never leave us nor forsake us, we should never allow ourselves to pine away — even for one hour — in this state. They who suffer in this way know all this, and they agree with it too. They know that God is able to uphold them; but it is another thing to possess the comfort of this assurance, to banish the night, and to break through the iron bars of the prison house.

What, we may ask, is "the end of the Lord" in placing us in such a furnace as this? This is too deep a question for our understanding in this life. Here, His footsteps are in the deep and His pathway in great waters. In the clearer light of eternity all our questions shall be answered, and there we shall see the wisdom and the love of God in all His dealings with us in this world of time.

A question, for example, which preoccupied the friends of Job was the background of his sufferings. Job, we know, suffered not for his sins, but for his holiness of life. His season of suffering marked the trial of his faith and patience; but he was not under God's rod of correction for some hidden transgression. In the eyes of God he was in his daily walk and conversation a "perfect and an upright man." To his friends, however, his trials, and the deep depression which came in their wake, were the tokens of God's anger and the play of His wrath against him for some hidden, unconfessed transgressions. According to them, Job's sin — whatever it was — had found him out. The deluge which swept over him was God's anger in operation. In the Book of Job the man who gives us the most consistent and Scriptural interpretation of Christian suffering — both before and after our conversion to God — is Elihu. Elihu's explanation of the sufferings of God's people was in reverse to that of the other three.

In his profound speech, Elihu envisages a man who is moving quite unconsciously towards spiritual disaster. The things of eternity give him no concern. He is going to live his life in his own way. God, however, arrests his way and opens his eyes to his danger. This He does in a twofold manner. The first is by an inward, mysterious unfolding of eternal realities. The second is by a devastating sickness and a prolonged season of pain. God warns him in a dream, and chastises him with His rod. Out of that school and ordeal a new man emerges. He stands before us clad in the garments of God's righteousness, enlightened by His Spirit and possessed of a new joy. In other words, God, by deep sufferings, destroyed the old earth-bound creature to make him a new man in Christ.

This is a picture of the way by which God sometimes brings sinners into a state of grace. It is also descriptive of the way in which the Lord deals with many of His people whom He hath chosen "in the furnace of affliction." He who has "his furnace in Jerusalem and his fire in Zion" often answers our prayers in such a way.

A man I knew once stood up to pray. He was a man who lived very near the Lord but one who also passed through great spiritual conflicts. He had been purged like gold and sifted as wheat. "Lord," he said, "some of us have, through the years, been praying for deeper holiness of life; but if we had known how our prayers were to be answered we might sometimes have withheld our voice." It was, in other words, by "fearful things" that the Lord answered his prayers.

Thomas Boston had a favourite verse. He wrote it at the beginning of his autobiography. "Thou who has showed me great and sore troubles shalt quicken me again and shalt bring me up again from the depths of the earth." In these words we see Hope in her night garments looking through the window of God's promise and waiting for the day. "Out of the depths have I cried unto thee, O Lord . . . . my soul waiteth for the Lord, more than they that watch for the morning . . . . Let Israel hope in the Lord for with the Lord is mercy . . . ."

Whatever their own fears, the Lord is never nearer to His people than when they are there lying low on the lap of such sorrows as these. "As one whom his mother comforteth, so will I comfort you." "When thou passest through the waters I shall be with thee." "He is touched with a feeling of our infirmity." One of the Puritan Fathers has well said that the Lord's people here are all in His hospital, and it is He who nurses each and all of them in their great affliction.

> "God will give strength when he on bed
> Of languishing doth mourn;
> And in his sickness sore, O Lord,
> Thou all his bed wilt turn."

Even when, under the weight of depression, they have no sense of His presence He is still there. His upholding hand is ever under them.

A Scottish minister was walking one night along a quiet country road. The night was clear and calm, and all the stars which beautified the sky seemed to smile on this lower world. In the way he met a little boy, and as they both looked toward the heavens the minister said, "How is it that the stars stay up there without falling?" "God," replied the thoughtful lad, "has a hold on them." This lovely and true saying from the lips of a mere child the minister often quoted as illustrating how, in sunshine and cloud, all the saints are in God's hand and are kept by His unfailing power.

One day I sat in a church in the town of Inverness, but of all that was said by the preacher that day I remember nothing apart from the one saying which, somehow, has remained in my mind with unfading clarity.

"God, as in the case of Psalmist, may bring His people down to the lowest pit, but however low they come, underneath them all are the everlasting arms." And as he said this, there were, I knew, some stricken hearts in the congregation which were touched by a deep sense of consolation.

These reassuring words remind me of a dear friend whose occasional letters I greatly valued, both for their deep spirituality and Christian sympathy. He was an English minister of the Evangelical Faith. For all I know, he may now be at his rest in heaven. In one of these he spoke of his prolonged spiritual trial; but he ended with the words, "Underneath are the everlasting arms." Many days passed before I heard from him again. Then one day I opened a letter in which he told me of his long day of trouble, and the letter ended with these same words: "Underneath are the everlasting arms." Those almighty arms of power and love were never, for a single moment, withdrawn from his soul. In all such trials, therefore, two things are certain. The anchor of our hope can never break, and the Rock to which it clings is eternal an unmoveable. Because our hope is in God and of God, we are safe. In the words of another, we may tremble on the Rock, but Christ, the Rock of Ages, is eternally the same. Against Him the gates of hell cannot prevail, and our faith in Him shares in the same victory. "For this is the victory that overcometh the world, even our faith."

If we had the power we would shield our loved ones from all pain and affliction. But, for higher and better ends, our Lord does not do this. His love and His afflicting hand are never incompatible. The one is the evidence of the other. It is, as we have remarked, in our pain and enfeeblement that we discover how deep and tender is His love, and how sufficient is His grace. The man who fell among thieves would never have discovered the depth of pity and love in the heart of his Samaritan friend had he not lain stricken in the way.

The three young men who were cast into the fiery furnace in Babylon had in the day of their trial the companionship of Him who was born for adversity. He shared their affliction and, in a way we cannot understand, transferred it to Himself. He transformed the furnace into a place of consolation. This is what we learn; that our greatest blessing, and our greatest discoveries of His love to us, comes through our greatest trials.

The late Mr Poole-Connor used to tell the story of an English lady, who lay in bed for many years. She was still a young woman, and also a follower of the Lord, when her health failed. The happy dreams which she had weaved of her future vanished under the shock of her sickness. For a season a great depression lay on her spirit. But one night she felt as if her Lord stood beside her and said, "I give you your trouble both for My glory and for your own good." These words served as a balm which reconciled her to God's hand. And it was through her affliction that He enriched her soul with His presence and promise.

Principal John MacLeod, of Inverness and Edinburgh, was fond of relating a remarkable sermon of a friend to whom he once listened. The sermon was on the way in which God may try His people in their hope. The preacher used an illustration. It was of a certain sea-bird which, by some instinctive urge, plunges from a great height into the depth of the sea. There it disappears, and anyone not familiar with its habits might conclude that

the sea had engulfed it for ever; but after a time it comes
to the surface and in its beak may be seen a live fish! In
the same way, he said, God's people are often brought
into the deep waters of affliction, but from these depths
God brings them up again with Christ alive in their soul
and His praise in their mouth. Job emerged out of such
depths with a song on his lips. "For I know that my
Redeemer liveth." From the bliss of the "third heaven"
Paul was brought down into conflict with the powers of
darkness, but in the end we hear him glorying in the
Lord, and also in his own weakness which linked him to
His almighty grace. "And He said unto me, my grace is
sufficient for thee . . . ." Those who, like him, have been
through these storms know that it truly is, for He Himself
lives within the grace which He gives day by day. "In
the Lord Jehovah is everlasting strength." "And as thy
day so shall thy strength be."

Is it not also a source of comfort to know that in all
such trials we are partakers of the sufferings of God's
people in every age? When we look into our Bibles,
there we see in the lives of the saints many of our own
experiences perfectly mirrored and described. For this
reason there is a bond of Christian affection and sympathy
between us and them. We also see that compared to
some of their afflictions ours are indeed light. A man
once quoted a Psalm which spoke both of the enjoyments
and of the afflictions of David. Then, as if speaking
personally to the Psalmist, he said, "O David, however
high I rise, you are above me, and however low I sink
you are still beneath me." Others, in other words, have
faced greater storms than we do; but each and all, whatever their encounters with adversity, were at last brought
into the desired haven.

A great source of comfort is to anticipate the day when the Lord shall withdraw every bitter cup and wipe away all tears from our eyes. Once I sat in a hospital at the bedside of a woman whose mind was under a heavy cloud of depression. As she mentioned some of her sufferings she said, "Heaven, I know, will be all the sweeter when this dark night is over." In contrast to our afflictions here the deep consolations of heaven, and the ever-deepening joys of an eternal day, shall be all the more wonderful.

In this chapter I mentioned the case of the one who, in the throes of spiritual distress, felt envious of those men who go in their way without concern with regard to their latter end. This excellent man is no longer with us. God has since taken him Home. A little while before his departure he appeared to his travelling friend in a remarkable dream. Sitting in a room together — as the dream was — they sang a verse of a Psalm:

> "Hear Lord, have mercy, help me, Lord,
> 　　Thou turned hast my sadness
> To dancing; yea, my sackcloth loosed
> 　　And girded me with gladness."　　　(Ps. 30).

As he sang these words the shadows of grief began to give way to a sudden and joyous transfiguration of his being. Darkness was being swallowed up in light. The dawn of Heaven had begun. The dream was prophetic, for within a short time he was across the river "with Christ which is far better." Sorrow and sighing had for ever fled away "Giant Despair" was no more.

> "The storm is changed into a calm
> 　　At his command and will
> So that the waves which raged before
> 　　Now quiet are and still."

CHAPTER VIII.

LONELINESS

WHEN God created man He endowed him with certain capacities and desires. He was created with the ability and the desire to enjoy fellowship with God and with other beings of his own kind. This was fundamental to his happiness. The social and spiritual aspects of his nature demanded this twofold communion.

Man, as God created him, was happy in fellowship with his Maker. God's blissful presence filled his soul with a deep peace. Each day came laden with new joys from the Fountain of all blessedness. The heavenly Sun shone upon him always. No cloud came between him and the Father of Lights.

But even in his state of sinless innocence "God saw that it was not good for man to be alone." As yet, man had no knowledge of, or communion with, beings on his own level of creation. In the quiet of that unfallen world he saw each beast and bird sharing life with their own kind and deeply satisfied in their own gregarious but irrational world; "but for man there was not found an helpmeet for him." This, perhaps, unconscious, want in his life God supplied. He brought on the scene one who was a perfect physical and spiritual counterpart of himself. At the moment the indefinable absence of that "something else" which man might have felt even in his unfallen state, disappeared. With it came a new joy — the joy of human companionship. This was an enrichment which must have deepened his happiness and integrated his divinely imparted social instincts.

Now, although sin has alienated us from God and from one another, it was part of God's purpose that, throughout eternity, we should still have communion with Himself and with one another "in the Lord." This was part of the purpose of redemption. Christ was to die that He might bring us together in Himself. He died that He might bring many sons and daughters to glory, and so fill every mansion in the New Jerusalem with those on whom He set His love. And next to communion with Himself, in that land of songs and smiles, communion with His people shall be the next best thing.

But in this fallen world of separation, sorrow and change, many of His people often tread the path of loneliness. One implication of their calling is that in the narrow way of truth, of holiness and devotion to God, few walk with them.

In one way, of course, God's people are never alone. He who loves them says in His word, "I will never leave thee, nor forsake thee." The intensity of this word **"never"** in the original Greek reminds us that God's love, God's power and God's covenant oath, all meet within this great promise and reassurance. The same wonderful love and promise are woven into another verse: "Lo, I am with you alway, even unto the end of the world." This is a promise which belongs to all the people of God in every age and to each one apart. It means that they are never alone — and never shall be.

This, however, does not mean that they enjoy an unbroken communion with Him in this world. There are, indeed, seasons of loneliness in the Christian life when the Beloved withdraws Himself. Times there are when clouds take Him out of their sight and when they mourn without the light of His face. God also speaks in His Word of the joy and value of Christian fellowship to those "who speak often the one to the other." It is a communion which He also shares; for He is there "in the midst." He listens to their conversations and perpetuates their thoughts of Him in His "Book of Remembrance."

The communion of the saints does not, however, require the bodily presence of one another. That cannot be; for it is something in another and a higher dimension. It belongs to the realm of the spirit. It is the union and communion of the mystical Body of Christ through Him who is the Head and who dwells in our hearts by faith. To think of Christian communion in terms of mere social contacts is to bring it down to the level of "things seen." Let me illustrate this fact by relating the following story.

A man once retired to his trysting place to pray. He lived in a community where he had little or no Christian fellowship with other believers. As this man stood before God a great sorrow filled his soul. "Lord," he whispered, "I am here where few call on Thy Name. Many who walked with Thee in other days are now with Thyself, and I am often alone." No sooner had he whispered these sad thoughts than he became aware that God, in a very real way, was speaking to him. "You are not alone, for I am here with you. And, besides, whatever hour of the night or day you kneel in My presence there are thousands of My people, scattered throughout the world, who are praying with you, and with whom you may have fellowship at the throne of grace." This gentle rebuke and reminder from the lips of the Lord made him bow his head. As the wonderful truth of what God had said dawned upon his mind, and as he breathed out his longings and desires before God, he knew, as never before, that he was only one of the great multitude whose prayers "like pillars of smoke" were ascending to heaven night and day. He knew also that he belonged to this great, if invisible, family of the Most High, for he felt his soul going out to them all in much love.

We are, therefore, never alone. In our glorious Mediator, and reconciled through His blood "we are come to Mount Zion unto the city of the living God, the heavenly Jerusalem, and to an innumerable company of angels, and to the general assembly and church of the firstborn which are written in heaven" (Heb. 12).

This spiritual communion does not, needless to say, bring into disparagement the assembling of ourselves together as the Lord commands. Christian fellowship, in "the body," is sweet and profitable. Paul had spiritual communion with the Lord's people, and yet he longed to see their face in the flesh. Our personal contacts often sweeten life, kindle our affections and greatly relieve our natural solitariness. Only in the heavenly country however, shall we be free from the loneliness which so often touches our life here.

In his old age, "the Apostle of the North," Doctor John MacDonald of Ferintosh, used to long for the company of those whom the Lord had taken Home, and in whose company his soul was so often refreshed on earth. God had removed from his side those dear companions of his earlier days, till at last he felt like a "solitary bird" whose fellows had taken wing to another and better clime.

One day, in a Highland parish, I stood listening to an old minister who prayed at the funeral service of a departed friend. "Lord," he said, "many of those whom we loved on earth are now with Thyself, and we long to be with them." But, in the words of another, "those who die in the Lord never say 'Farewell' for the last time." We shall meet again — very soon.

Not only are the Lord and His people with us here in the spirit, but as the Word of the Lord teaches, we are also favoured with the invisible, and often unconscious ministry and presence of His holy angels, "ye are come . . . . to an innumerable company of angels." These are given charge to keep us in all our ways. This is a great Scriptural promise of which we should never lose sight. If we are heirs of salvation we are provided with guardians who keep us till we pass out of this imperilled and dangerous world. Do we ever think of this as we should? Just as our Queen has her secret guardians as she moves from place to place, so Christ's Bride is provided with an invisible and sure protection as she journeys Home through this world.

Let me give one example of the comfort which should reach us through God's care of us in this mysterious way. One night a man retired to rest. It was winter, and he lived in a lonely hollow with no one very near. As he lay down to sleep a great fear clutched at his heart, for in the next room a loved one was weak and ill. What if he took ill, too? The winter months were creeping in upon them, and if he took ill what would happen? Then sleep touched his eyes. When, in the early morning, he awoke he felt that God was beside him; and He had come with the gift of a much needed promise in these words:

"No plague shall near thy dwelling come,
　　No ill shall thee befall,
　For thee to keep in all thy ways
　　His angels charge He shall."

(Ps. 91, v. 10-11).

During the grim days of that long winter he used these words as a staff in his hand. Others, he knew, were there with him. The Great Guardian of His Israel had provided the needed help. Both He and His angels were there night and day.

The late Principal John MacLeod used to tell the story of an excellent woman whose godly husband was dying of a dangerous and contagious infection. As he lay down in his couch to die his wife was alone, for in the circumstances her neighbours were afraid to enter her home. As her beloved husband breathed his last a sense of great loneliness filled her spirit. "Lover and friend Thou has put far from me." These words of the Psalmist she sobbed out of her broken heart before God. It was then that she heard a voice: "You are alone, woman." It was then also that she saw an impressive stranger, who quietly entered her room. After he had carefully attended to the precious remains he sat with her by the fire. But not another word did he speak. With the break of day he took his leave. The man had brought heaven into her home, for as he sat there beside her all fears and sense of loneliness left her. Instead, she knew that she was one of a great multitude over whom Death had no real power, and who were destined to live eternally in God's presence where her loved one now was. She never saw her visitor before or after; but the afterglow of his very presence seemed to tarry in her home for many days. And though our eyes may not see those who surround us in the crises of life they are truly there.

So far as human companionship is concerned loneliness is something which has touched the lives of God's people in every age. There have been periods in the history of the Church of God when many of God's people had to walk in a solitary way. They were like lone stars in the prevailing darkness, or like rare plants who graced the moral and spiritual deserts which surrounded them.

Let us look for a moment at how some of God's choice saints had to live and witness in other days. Enoch, for example, had no companion on earth but God Himself. Although he apparently lived a normal family life in his own community he was, spiritually, a man apart. Like his Lord while here "the world knew him not," and he refused to know the evil, unbelieving world of his day. His great descendant, Noah, was also a lone voice and witness in his terrible age. He kept out of the paths wherein destroyers go. The world had become a moral dunghill, but his holy life was untouched by the pollutions of his time. The multitudes who moved toward physical and eternal destruction resented his prophetic warnings and disparaged his entire devotion to God. Holiness and loneliness often go together. If we fit into the world pattern many are with us. But our Christian consecration is too rich a jewel to lose in the world's mire.

As we move forward through the centuries, the same story is repeated many times. In his native city of Ur, Abraham was just one of its pagan population. He was perfectly at home amid the idolatries and spiritual ignorance of the crowd. But the moment God whispered His saving Word into his soul he became a stranger and a pilgrim on the earth. When God embraced him as His friend he immediately, and forever, left the haunts of sin. This was the implication of his call and the hallmark of his faith.

There are few stories in the Bible so rich in pathos as the story of Jacob who, after the shades of night had fallen around him, lay down to sleep at Bethel. Who can describe his loneliness that night, as he rested his weary head on a stone? The previous day he had said a fond farewell to his father and mother. But the homeless wanderer God adopted and espoused. "The Lord is in this place; this is God's house, and this is the gate of heaven." Holy beings from another and fairer world surrounded the green slope on which he lay his head. God was to be his Companion for evermore. On his death-bed he spoke wistfully and lovingly of the "Angel" who kept him all his days, and into whose eternal Home he was about to enter.

Many of God's people today dwell in communities where loneliness and fear are seldom absent. But their trials are small compared to a man like Lot who, in those cities of terror, was alone. As God's providence revealed, neither his wife nor his family had the fear of God in their hearts. But the Lord who loved him gave His angels charge concerning him to keep him in all his ways.

Many centuries after this we find one of God's prophets describing his own times and his own loneliness, not only in the society of his day but within the visible Church. "The good man is perished out of the earth; and there is none upright among men . . . . Therefore will I look to the Lord." Of all whom he knew on earth there was no one to whom he could look for help, for sympathy and understanding.

How well does the late Doctor Tozer of America express the nature and cause of the loneliness of the saints. "The loneliness of the Christian results from his walk with God in an ungodly world, a walk that must often take him away from the fellowship of good Christians as well as from that of the unregenerate world.

His God-given instincts cry out for companionship with others of his kind, others who can understand his longings, his aspirations, his absorption in the love of Christ; and because within his circle of frends there are so few who share his inner experiences he is forced to walk alone. The unsatisfied longings of the prophets for human understanding caused them to cry out in their complaint, and even our Lord Himself suffered in the same way.

"The man who has passed on into the divine Presence in actual inner experience will not find many who understand him. A certain amount of social fellowship will, of course, be his as he mingles with religious persons in the regular activities of the church, but true spiritual fellowship will be hard to find. But he should not expect things to be otherwise. After all, he is a stranger and a pilgrim, and the journey he takes is not on his feet but in his heart. He walks with God in the garden of his own soul — and who but God can walk there with him? He is of another spirit from the multitudes that tread the courts of the Lord's house.

"The truly spiritual man is indeed something of an oddity. He lives not for himself but to promote the interests of Another. He seeks to persuade people to give all to his Lord, and asks no portion or share for himself. He delights not to be honoured but to see his Saviour glorified in the eyes of men. His joy is to see his Lord promoted and himself neglected.

"He finds few who care to talk about that which is the supreme object of his interest, so he is often silent and preoccupied in the midst of noisy religious shop-talk. For this he earns the reputation of being dull and over-serious, so he is avoided and the gulf between him and society widens. He searches for friends upon whose garments he can detect the smell of myrrh and aloes and cassia out of the ivory palaces, and finding few or none he, like Mary of old, keeps these things in his heart.

"It is this very loneliness that throws him back upon God. 'When my father and my mother forsake me, then the Lord will take me up.' His inability to find human companionship drives him to seek in God what he can find nowhere else."

If we, like such men, enjoyed a deeper sense of God's presence in our daily walk the absence of human companionship, however helpful in other ways, we would gladly endure. When He is with us all loneliness is gone. We heard of a man who was once walking in the way, apparently alone. But he was very, very happy with the presence of God in his soul. At that moment he could say, "Whom have I in heaven but thee? And there is none on earth that I desire beside thee." It was then that he heard someone behind him remarking affably, "Well, you are alone." As he turned round to look at the unwelcome person who had disturbed his communion with God he said in a sad voice, "Yes, I am alone now." This, then, is what we should pray for, and value above all earthly friendship — the conscious presence of the Beloved on the way Home.

But these enjoyments come and go. To His own He is often like a wayfaring man who turneth aside to tarry for a night.

Our Lord Himself knew the path of loneliness while He was here. He was an unwanted Stranger in this world. "I am a stranger to my brethren and an alien to my mother's children." On earth, we know, He enjoyed constant communion with God the Father. Angels ministered to Him in His need and sufferings. But He always anticipated that dread hour when all His earthly friends would forsake Him. "Ye shall leave Me alone; yet I am not alone for the Father is with Me." The hour arrived, however, when in utter desolation He was removed an infinite distance not only from men but from God also. The cry of dereliction on the cross of Calvary, "My God, My God, why hast Thou forsaken Me?" was riven through with an agony and a pain which none of His people shall ever know. At that moment a dread unspeakable loneliness which His people would otherwise have to endure for ever was present in His consciousness in all its stark reality. Unlike His, **our** loneliness here — as we have tried to show — is more apparent than real; and in whatever degree it touches our lives we may be assured of His sympathy and care. Whatever path we travel in He was there before us. And wherever we are, and however we are, He has promised to be to each one of us "a little sanctuary" till we reach the mansions of glory.

Our comparative loneliness here is, however, a fit preparation for that unending communion with Himself which we shall soon enjoy. The believer on the way to Heaven may be likened to the bride in the old world story whose husband had asked her to join him in another and better country. The voyage thither was long, and a feeling of loneliness often touched her heart. But the hope of seeing the loved one on the other side sustained her spirit to the end. In the same way God's people rejoice in the day when they shall see their Lord face to face. "But ye now have sorrow: but I will see you again and your heart shall rejoice, and your joy no man shall take from you."

Let us, in the light of Scripture, envisage what this

arrival in heaven would mean to any of God's solitary people. In a moment the tie between soul and body is dissolved. In that same instant they are present with the Lord, and among "the great congregation" who stand faultless before the Throne. Their Lord, the Beloved of their soul, they now see without a cloud between. How it happens, they cannot tell. It is all a miracle of God's power and love. We look, and there also we see and know those whom we loved in the Lord on earth. All loneliness is forever gone: we are in our blissful and Eternal Home.

"They shall be brought with gladness great
        And mirth on every side,
Into the palace of the King,
        And there they shall abide."

(Ps. 45, v. 15).

CHAPTER IX.

" THE CROOK IN THE LOT "

" THE CROOK IN THE LOT " is the title of a famous book written by Thomas Boston. There are few autobiographical disclosures more impressive than Thomas Boston's references to his well-beloved wife. She was a woman who knew the grace of God in truth. Her deep love of her Redeemer endeared her greatly to her husband. The depth of Boston's affection for his wife was, however, associated with a sorrow and a compassion which he could never express in mere words. Over a long period of their life together his dear one was insane. There were seasons when he had to retire to an adjoining "outhouse" to conceal his distress from his family, while she lay in what he called "the inner prison." Yet, no word of complaint ever fell from his lips. This was because in Boston's soul there was a bright and sure hope that their trial was but the prelude to a happy eternity for them both. Out of this womb of sorrow came his great work mentioned above. God turned his trial into a ministry of comfort to untold thousands of His people.

Boston knew that in this life there is no nest without its thorn. To envisage an undisturbed rest all our days here is not wise. God's people, the subjects of His love and care, had in every age a cup of sorrow put into their hand. The first man who ever exercised a living faith in God in this world was the subject of his brother's malice. Cain hated Abel for no other reason than that God loved him and that he loved his God, and that, unlike himself, his life and worship were both acceptable to his Maker. From that hour, and in every age, God's people could say, "For Thy sake we are killed all the day."

Some may believe that their sorrows are unique, and that others lie in quieter pastures than themselves. With the prophet they ask, "Is there any sorrow like unto my sorrow?" But we seldom know the inner nature of our neighbour's sorrow. And as Boston reminds us, the sources of these sorrows — whether known or unknown to others — often lie on our own hearth. A fit comment on this truth is the well-known story of a good woman who believed that her own domestic trial was more unbearable than that of her pious neighbours, and whose heart God set at ease in a remarkable dream. She dreamt that, passing through the village where she stayed, she saw opposite each door the burdens which each of her friends had to bear. She lifted each one to her back, only to discover that no burden fitted her but the one which lay at her own door! Out of all the burdens of woe which lay before her, she was led, after much reflection, to choose her own. God, in other words, had adapted her burden to her ability to bear it. This is what we learn. He will not try us beyond our endurance. His disciplines are perfectly weighed and measured by His wisdom and love, and are peculiarly fitted for the end He has in view for each and all of His people — their final consolation and perfection. Sin has wrought so many evil twists in our nature that there can be no straightening of our lives without the needed and appropriate pain. It is not willingly, therefore, that He afflicts the children of men, and especially those who are the subjects of unchanging love.

The famous Dr Kennedy of Dingwall once said that all the afflictions meted out for us by God in that covenant "which is ordered in all things and sure" He will put into the cup of our daily experience. Since all He gives is for His own glory, and for our own good, not a drop more shall be added to that cup, and not a drop less shall be withheld. And when, in a spirit of acceptance and resignation, we uncomplainingly take it out of His hand, our will is beginning to dovetail into His. This is the secret of inner peace. But, oh, what grace is needed to say, "Not my will, but Thine be done."

In one of his great afflictions the Psalmist wished for the wings of a dove that he might fly away to where he might rest. But not till all the sorrows which beset us here pass away shall our souls take wing to that sweet land where grief is unknown. Meanwhile let us pray for the needed grace that shall enable us to endure to the end. And if our sufferings, in some measure, are due to an attachment to Christ great indeed are our honour and privilege. A story was once rehearsed in a small company of Christian people of a certain man who, bearing a sore cross, went aside to pray. He would have the Lord remove his burden. When he arose from his knees he felt that his plea was refused. That night a young man stood beside him with an open Bible in his hand. With great solemnity he read the words: "Unto you it is given in the behalf of Christ, not only to believe in Him, but also to suffer for His sake." Through these words he realised anew that the way of blessedness is to be found in acceptance of God's holy will for us in whatever He calls upon us to endure.

As illustrative of God's ability to sustain us under our sharpest trials, the following story is not without its value and instruction.

Many years ago a group of Christian men were working in a certain district. They were men who greatly valued the means of grace. They were also men of much spiritual discernment. Each Lord's Day they sat in the local church listening to a comparatively young minister of the Gospel. As they listened they were amazed at his spiritual maturity, and at the tenderness with which he proclaimed his message. He was the friend and comforter of the afflicted soul. One day, one of the men ventured to ask him where he had learned these deep lessons in Christian sufferings and the fruits they bear. "If," he said, "you will come with me to my home I shall let you know." This they did. After they had eaten of the meal which he had prepared, he said, "Come now, and I shall show you where I got my sermon." He led them to a room where they saw, tied to its bed, a deformed and retarded child. And in another room lay a woman — his wife — in a drunken stupor. As they walked away they knew how true was the Word of the Lord in relation to many of His own, "Thou hast showed Thy people hard things; Thou hast made us to drink the wine of astonishment."

A similar story could indeed be told of another excellent man who laboured for many years in a Scottish parish. Sometimes, in the night, this man would yoke his horse and search the ditches by the wayside for his foolish son whom, he knew, had fallen by the way. The cry of David, "O Absalom, my son! my son!" was one which must have often wrenched his spirit. God, however, gave him the needed strength for his burden, and out of the furnace he emerged refined by the presence of the One "who was born for adversity."

God can truly use the path of pain as a means of blessing. The hard things which so often crush our lives may be the tokens of His love and the channel through which we enjoy more of His grace. "By these things men live, and in these is the life of the spirit." "As many as I love, I rebuke and chasten." As Boston reminds us, one reason why the Lord brings some of His people into the path of adversity is that they might know how to comfort others "with the comfort wherewith themselves are also comforted of God."

During my earlier years in the ministry I knew two men who each bore a heavy cross in his home. When they stood up in public, either to witness or to pray, one could discern how deeply God had taught them in the school of affliction. Once they met, and as they greeted one another, they both wept. They wept in mutual sympathy and understanding; for their crosses were identical. Each understood the nature and the sharpness of the thorn which wrung the heart of the other. They were men who knew how to minister comfort to burdened souls.

As an example of how God can sweeten life's bitter waters, we recall the words of a Highland Divine, the holy Mr Fraser of Alness, in Ross-shire. Till he breathed his last this man's unbelievably cruel wife would deny him both his necessary food and the minimum comfort of his home. But to him she was "the best wife in the world," for each day as he kneeled under his burden, God, through His promise, assured him of His unfailing love and that His grace would always be sufficient.

To those whose path here is often strewn with such sharp thorns, there is a promise that has often been fulfilled in the experience of many of His people. It is that God, by a work of grace, is able to change those who may oppress us. The prophet, in figurative words, speaks of the great and lasting change which God's saving power can bring about in the lives of men. "Instead of the thorn shall come up the fir tree, and instead of the briar shall come up the myrtle tree, and it shall be to the Lord for a name, for an everlasting sign that shall not be cut off." The serpent from which Moses once recoiled in fear afterwards became a staff in his hand. God can change the sources of our sorrows into a means of strength and comfort. Let me elucidate this great truth by one or two examples.

I once knew an excellent Christian man whose wife was also a jewel of God's grace. Three times a day they both kneeled together in prayer at the family altar. The Bible was always open on their little fireside table. Never did I enter that tiny cottage with its "but-and-ben," without the feeling that the Lord was there. But it had not always been so. The man whom I took — at my first acquaintance with him — to have been a Samuel from the womb, had once been the heartbreak of his wife. When drink and ill-temper took possession of him he became a destroyer of his home and a terror to his lovely and devoted spouse. God, however, saw her tears and heard her prayer, and their last years in this world were lived in the quiet assurance of God's love and forgiveness.

Let me describe another such home. Once I stood outside a church in one of our cities. Out of the crowd a man approached me and asked me to his home. There a goodly company sat down at his table, which was followed by family worship. This man was a very joyous believer. He was like one who had found great spoil or

had suddenly lighted on a hid treasure. His happy wife
was the willing Martha of his home. When, in a kindly
way, I chided with him for placing such a burden on her,
as our visit entailed, he looked at me earnestly, and in a
voice full of sorrow he said, "There was a day when I
was hard on my wife . . ." Afterwards I heard the story
of his reckless years, and of her broken heart and home.
Now her sighs had given place to smiles, while he never
wearied of telling what God had done for him in "a day
of His power."

How applicable are the words of Solomon with regard
to the grief which is so often found in the hearts of many
parents. "A foolish son is the heaviness of his mother."
A young man whom I once knew seemed to live for no
other thing than to bring misery into his home. He boxed
his compass in his own foolish way. After years of
ploughing his deep furrows of ill-conduct he arrived one
evening in church where he sat beside his father whose
prayers on his behalf had, we believed, at last prevailed
with God.

A minister once preached a sermon in which he exhorted those of his hearers who "sowed in tears" not to
forget the promise that they would "reap with joy." He
told a remarkable story of a Christian man whose sons
made light of their Christian upbringing and heritage,
and who went on carelessly in the hard way of trans-
gressors. Over the long years their father prayed for their
salvation; but he passed into God's presence with his
prayers apparently unanswered. Then he died, and his
wayward sons followed his dust to the grave. On that
day, as they entered the home of their early years, they
saw the old, tear-stained chair beside which their father
so often kneeled in prayer for them. As they stood there

in silence something like a wave out of the eternal world touched their spirits and compelled them to fall down on their knees and to ask God for mercy. From that hour they were new men in Christ. Their subsequent life of devotion to the cause of Christ was ample proof that God had richly answered their father's prayers.

These things do happen. They teach us that we should pray for those who oppress us. There are those who taste of such joys of prayers answered on earth, and, for reasons of His own, there are those whose prayers meantime remain unanswered and whom the Lord leaves here all their days with afflictions which pierce deeper and deeper into their spirits. But "God is not slack concerning His promise." Only in the world to come shall many see how their prayers on behalf of those who had so often grieved them here, did prevail with God. And these sweet surprises "within the veil" shall add to their cup of joy.

Meantime He says, "My grace is sufficient for thee . . . ." "All things work together for good to those who love Him." If our earthly lot is therefore hedged in with many sorrows, let us remember that there is a lot without a crook, and a blessing to which no sorrow is added. How wonderful are the words of the Psalm:

> "God is of mine inheritance
> And cup the portion;
> The lot that fallen is to me
> Thou dost maintain alone."

Besides, our season of pain is but for "a little while." The years of our mourning shall cease. The tears which sometimes dim our eyes He shall shortly wipe away.

A few years ago a man sat in a church. In front of him he could see a company of men who were the local

elders. He knew them well; he also knew something of
the trials which some of them had to endure. Some of
them were men on whose hearts the shadows of sorrow
lay. When the service had ended he went over and stood
among them. "Cheer up, friends," he said, "the worst is
over, and the best is yet to be." He meant that their
voyage on life's sea was now almost over and that the
blissful shore of a better world was already in view.
They all understood and smiled. The sure hope is
beautifully expressed in the Psalm:

> "Weeping may for a night endure,
> At morn doth joy arise."

Let me conclude this chapter with the story of an
eminent Christian man who once "spoke to the Question."
The man ended his remarks by saying that whatever
bitter herbs God's people may have to taste in this life
there was one herb which would never lose its sweetness.
He then sat down. Immediately the presiding minister
stood up and said: "Perhaps our friend might tell us
what this sweet herb is." The man arose, and with great
tenderness, quoted the words: "Jesus Christ, the same
yesterday, to-day and for ever." The words, needless to
say, came with much comfort to many present.

CHAPTER X.

FRUSTRATION

LIVING in a world of opposition to God and His Cause it is inevitable that God's people, on whatever level they seek to serve Him, should often be overtaken by a sense of frustration. Their sphere of labour may be large or small: it may be in the secret place, or carried on in the presence of men; but one thing is certain — the enemy is there to oppose them. If the Lord opens doors of usefulness for them there are many adversaries who try to close them.

The desire to serve the Lord is uppermost in the heart of every one of Christ's sincere followers. With another they say, "Lord, what wilt Thou have me to do?" This desire is born of a sense of indebtedness to the One Who did so much for them. Sometimes they wistfully dream of the goodly harvest which they hope to reap before life's brief day is over. Like King David, who had hoped to build a house for the Lord, they pray that their fond expectation may have its fulfilment before they leave this scene of time. Their morning of hope is often bright, but as the day lengthens towards its close they begin to realise how little they have done. Behind them they see a long furrow of broken and unprofitable service. With another they say, "I have laboured in vain, I have spent my strength for nought."

These words of the prophet remind us of a devoted servant of the Lord who laboured long and faithfully in a certain Scottish district. He began his work full of lively expectations. He had hoped that all who listened to the Good News would believe, and that all who professed to believe would help forward God's work by their prayers and outward diligence. He was looking for spiritual Aarons and Hurs who would continually uphold his hands in the Lord's work. But like many another he soon made the discovery that within the Church on earth there were three types. There were those who did nothing. They either stood idle all the day, or often did the reverse of what they ought to do. There were also those who did the necessary incumbent task, and no more. And there were those rare and choice souls who, like Mary, did all they could for their Lord. With all the discouragements which came his way this good man sobbed these words out of a broken heart: "I have laboured in vain!"

Many others have walked in the same way. They discover that for every one who is on the Lord's side a hundred are in the other camp. We know that the great Adversary and his emissaries never rest in their opposition to Christ and His kingdom. Judas and his friends slept not in the solemn hour of Christ's crisis and sorrow. But His disciples did. And while we sleep Satan sows his tares. Ever since the Lord lighted the candle of Truth in the world, there has been, on the part of His enemies, a continuous attempt to quench its flames; and if we look at the pages of history we see how often they almost succeeded.

A famous Scottish preacher once remarked that over the long years of the divine forbearance Noah's hammer continued to preach to a lost world. "Repent," "Return," was its incessant voice. But no one heeded. The multitudes whom he warned passed on to eternal destruction. He made no converts outside his own family. Elijah, one of his great successors in the faith, lay down in a fit of despair and prayed that he might die. A nation which God had embraced as His own had degenerated into a state of rebellion and idolatry, and preferred to listen to the swarms of false prophets who preached "smooth things" and followed their own vision. And throughout that long spiritual night many of his faithful successors passed through the same experience. Such seasons of frustration do not belong to what some describe as the obstinate, primitive ages of the past. They belong to this Gospel age as well.

One can imagine, for example, with what bright anticipation did John the Baptist move away from the bank of the river on that day when he saw the Holy Dove resting on the Person of his Lord, and when he heard God's voice from heaven testifying to His pleasure in His own dear Son. God had personally entered the world, and all power in heaven and on earth was given to Him. Surely Satan would now retreat to his own dark abode, and his followers would soon be brought low. The Sun was risen and would go down no more! Within a short time, however, John was asking the heart-rending question, "Art thou he that should come, or do we look for another?" What had happened? John was in prison; and the One whom he took to be the Lord of Glory was meeting with disparagement and opposition in His own nation. His question was born of fear. If our Lord's answer finally convinced him that Satan, "the strong man armed," could no longer keep his goods in peace because a greater was now on the scene, he himself went to his death the victim of the world's malice.

An incident is recorded in the Gospel which may illustrate the sense of frustration which often overtakes those who would serve the Lord and become fishers of men. It is the story of the disciples' night of toil on the lake of Gennesaret. "Master, we have toiled all the night and have taken nothing." The fish were there, the nets were cast, and the season was opportune, but they had nothing to show for the long toil of the night.

Is this not the way with many in our own day? Earnest men and women, by prayer and witnessing, seek to rescue souls out of their spiritual plight; but they see not their signs. Their prayers are apparently unheard and their work unblessed. Many of God's servants toil on, afraid that they are but "unprofitable servants." But this is exactly what the Lord wants them to say, for it is something that the graceless, unsent hirelings would never say. These are, as a rule, pleased enough with themselves and with their own work.

We mentioned on one or two of those who laboured and sorrowed in other days. But, for our own comfort, let us look at their work in retrospect. Did they really labour in vain? Where do they stand? We speak rather foolishly of "success," but the Lord speaks of "faithfulness." Their faithfulness was what God valued and rewarded. "Well done, thou good and faithful servant: enter thou into the joy of thy Lord." "Because thou hast kept the word of My patience, I also will keep thee from the hour of temptation which shall come upon all the earth . . ." In terms of converts Noah had "failed"; but as a faithful witness against evil, and on the side of righteousness, he was a spiritual star of the first magnitude. By his faith and its works Noah "condemned the world" and preserved the holy seed through whom, in the Person of our Lord and His people, the world was to be redeemed and God's cause preserved to the end of time. His was a life of triumph over the forces of darkness and destruction. Because of his faith in God, men and women still breathe on this planet! If his own age disparaged his witness and mocked his work, successive generations bless God for what he did and for what he was. In an age of moral contamination he defiled not his garments. In contrast to a world that had become a moral dunghill he was like a flower whose fragrance of holiness still wafts through its very air.

If the world of David, Elijah and Isaiah was somewhat less terrible than that of Noah it produced the same sense of frustration in the minds of those who served the Lord. The enemy continued to come in like a flood; but a man like Elijah had not failed when he wished for death. In the gathering darkness and spiritual deterioration of his age, it was he who kept the lamp of Truth from going out and who passed it on to the generations to come.

And what shall we say of the Prophet's cry, "I have laboured in vain, I have spent my strength for nought"? When Isaiah uttered these words he was no doubt sincere at the bar of his own experience. Throughout his prophetic ministry he had warned his nation against its evil ways, and proclaimed the great positive truths of the Gospel with no uncertain voice. But his ministry was exercised among a people whose ears were deaf and whose eyes were blind. And God brought them under His judgment for their persistent unconcern and unbelief. But whatever discouragement he met with he continued his ministry of prayer and preaching. Listen to his words. "There is none that calleth on thy name, and stirreth up himself to lay hold upon thee . . . . And I will wait upon the Lord that hideth his face from the house of Jacob, and I will look for him."

Did he labour in vain? Think for a moment of the vast multitudes who, through the blessing of God, have found their way into the realms of eternal bliss through his God-given ministry. And this will go on to the end of time. How many have found the river of life through his words, "Ho, everyone that thirsteth, come ye to the waters"? How many have found eternal reconciliation and peace through his lifting up of a crucified Redeemer? "He is brought as a lamb to the slaughter and as a sheep before her shearers is dumb, so he opened not his mouth . . . He shall see of the travail of his soul, and shall be satisfied."

The truth is that in this life the results of our labours are largely unknown. "Their works do follow them." Heaven, as we have said, is a place of joyous surprises. There we shall see "what God hath wrought" through our poor and often despised labours. The toil of the night shall be followed by the joy of the day, when "on the other side" we shall see the fruit of our toil. There-fore "let us not be weary in well-doing, for in due season we shall reap if we faint not." "They that sow in tears shall reap in joy."

Every worker for the Lord should draw comfort from the fact that he or she is on the winning side. God's enemies have no future and no promise of success. The devil is not only under His heel but under our feet also. "And the God of peace shall bruise Satan under your feet shortly." However formidable the foes, and however pervasive their influence in our age, they and their works shall perish. Satan and his slaves, with all the channels through which they invade the souls of men and defile our world, shall be removed. "The meek shall inherit the earth," and by their devotion to God's will, and through the outpouring of God's Spirit in answer to their prayers, the earth shall yet be filled with the glory of the Lord "as the waters cover the sea." This is our hope. If to-day our Gospel is "counted as a very small thing" tomorrow the Good News shall be welcomed throughout the whole earth.

The bread which we meantime cast upon the waters shall return to us, not immediately, but "after many days." We kneel, for example, at the Throne of Grace and pray for the race that is to come and for the children who are yet unborn. Meantime we pass on into God's presence; but our prayers He will continue to answer. The secret prayers of the Church are like precious stones gently dropped into the ocean of Eternity. They produce waves which shall one day touch unknown shores, and return laden with blessings to future generations. A law operates in the physical world whereby even the sounds of a tiny bell move into the unknown immensities of outer space. And the prayers of the Church of Christ move into the deep dimensions of the eternal world and reach the ear of God. The man or woman who, unknown to the world, kneels before God in prayer, God shall reward together with those who labour openly before men. At Jesus' feet Mary was silent, apart from her tears, but her Lord said, "She hath done what she could." Her silent ministry of love towards His Person and His cause was the unfading memorial which she left behind her. If her name is in God's Book here on earth God has another Book in Heaven wherein is recorded the labours of all His people. This Book of Remembrance — which someone has spoken of as God's Diary — perpetuates the thoughts, conversations and all the secret service of His people here. Nothing shall be forgotten, for God is not unrighteous to forget their work and their labours of love "shown toward His name." If their labours are ignored, forgotten, or even unknown here, His word holds out the promise that the memorial of the righteous is for ever.

The history of the Church is replete with evidences that the fulfilment of God's promise is always linked to the prayers of His people. In Old Testament times the prayers of the Church were ascending to heaven "like pillars of smoke" for the promised day when the Sun of Righteousness would arise on this world "with healing in His wings." Christ related the coming of the Spirit in Pentecostal power to the prayers of His waiting people. During the age of papal darkness in Europe there were those who continued to witness throughout that long spiritual night. These, by their faith, anticipated the happy day when the true Church of Christ would come back to the origins of our faith and rediscover her Lord and His Gospel in His own holy Word. And those who are loyal to Christ to-day, however discouraged they may often feel through the oppositions and distractions of this terrible age, shall not be forgotten in the days to come when God "shall bring His sons from afar and His daughters from the ends of the earth." "When the Lord shall build up Zion, He shall appear in His glory. He will regard the prayer of the destitute . . . This shall be written for the generation to come; and the people which shall be created shall praise the Lord."

The famous "Mr Lachlan" Mackenzie of Lochcarron once spoke in figurative language of the prayers of God's people as the "coins" which, day after day, at the Throne of Grace they present to God. Each valued "coin" or prayer is received at the heavenly Bank. And one day all shall return into their hand and heart with God's full interest added thereto. Men therefore "ought always to pray and not to faint." "The Lord doth reign." "He shall not fail nor be discouraged until he hath set up righteousness in the earth, and the isles shall wait for His law." "And let us not be weary in well doing; for in due season we shall reap if we faint not."

CHAPTER XI

TOMORROW'S CARES

ONE of the mysteries of life concerns the recognised difference between worldly men and the people of God. Although the former pitch their tent on the brink of destruction they are often, not only where eternal issues are concerned but also in relation to their life here, comparatively free from care. In relation to the unknown future within the circle of God's providence the righteous may, on the other hand, be full of anxious care.

This was the mystery which exercised the mind of Asaph when he envied some of "the foolish" who seemed to live under the smile of a kindly providence. No cup of sorrow was in their hand. They were clad in the garments of pride. They prospered in the world. God seemed to leave them alone, while they dismissed Him from their thoughts as One Who was remote from, and irrelevant to, the kind of life they wished to live.

In one of His parables our Lord speaks of this type — so familiar in real life. This man had no care. The future of his own imagination was all fair and benign. Although Death was already at his door he was thinking wistfully over his worldly success and of the many years of enjoyment which were yet to come. God addressed this man as "a fool." But only God did. In his own eyes and in the eyes of his fellow men he had attained to "security" and success. How often have we seen such!

Bunyan's **Atheist**, with his back to God, laughed as he stumbled into perdition. To him there was no world worth seeking but the present. In fact, there was none other to seek.

Asaph solved this mystery of providence before God in prayer. He relates the whole experience in Psalm seventy-three. He saw how deceptive were mere appearances. The carefree man of the world became suddenly shrouded in darkness, while the trembling saint guided and upheld by an omnipotent, if invisible, hand, he saw passing into the eternal serenities of God's presence.

But the theme of this chapter is not so much the bewilderment which the dispensations of God's providence may sometimes create in our mind; but rather the danger of anticipating our trials and of letting the cares of this life oppress us too heavily.

Our Lord exhorted His people to be careful for nothing, and not to endure beforehand the trials which have not yet arrived. "Take no thought for the morrow, for the morrow shall take thought for the things of itself." "Sufficient unto the day is the evil thereof."

These words do not mean that we are to exclude all necessary and reasonable preparation for the future from our thinking. The Christian is not a fatalist who, like a Moslem Arab, folds his hands and does nothing. There is a legitimate care as there is a sinful anxiety. It is this anxious preoccupation with an unknown future against which our Lord warns us. For one thing tomorrow is veiled from our eyes. We know not what a day, or even an hour may bring forth. God alone knows the future in its entirety. How many tomorrows have we envisaged in the past? But few, if any of them, fitted into the pattern of our imagination. The bridges which we expected to cross long ago we have not yet reached? The insupportable trials, the overcoming temptations, the crushing burdens, which we so often feared have still to arrive. And arrive, as such, they never shall if our trust is in the Lord and His grace. To place to-morrow's cares on the top of today's is a burden too heavy for our mortal frame. Let us also remember that although the grace of God is always sufficient and ever available it is not given in advance. "As thy days, so shall thy strength be." Doctor Payson once said, "antici-pated sorrows are harder to bear than real ones, because Christ does not support us under them." Whatever the future may bring God will adapt His strength to every situation. With the need — and only then — comes His grace. This promise is in the present tense. This grace was not given to Paul in the third heaven — a few hours before the trial came. It was given in answer to prayer when Satan had arrived at his door.

This promise of grace in all the crises of life should indeed, calm our spirits. A person I know went to bed one night full of anxiety. The tasks and expected trials of the coming days, along with his own sense of weakness, lay heavily on his spirit. Then, like the chime of a distant bell, these words of a Psalm became articulate within his soul:

> "O, why art thou cast down, my soul,
>   What could discourage thee?
> And why with vexing thoughts are thou
>   Disquieted in me?
> Still trust in God; for Him to praise
>   Good cause I yet shall have;
> He of my countenance is the health,
>   My God that doth me save."

Then the dark forebodings in which he clothed the coming days took their departure.

One reason why we should leave tomorrow in God's hand is that, long before he created us, He arranged the content of each day. Nothing, therefore, is haphazard or left to chance. All that happens within the sphere of His providence is as unchangeable as His love. Because, then, our times are in His hand — present and future — we should be content with whatever the present may bring or the future may disclose. "Be content with such things as ye have; for He hath said, I will never leave thee nor forsake thee."

Once I thought that these words meant that we should rest content with the smallest tokens of His goodness and mercy towards us in this life. But the words have a fuller meaning. He commands us to be content with our cares and with all our burdens. Why? Because "He hath said, I will never leave thee nor forsake thee." This is what more than compensates for every trial. His own promised presence with us in the days to come is the guarantee that all shall be well. This should sweeten the unknown future, and resign us to His will.

The spiritual peace and detachment which reign in our hearts when we acquiesce in the will of God is spoken of by David under a figure which is as tender as it is significant. "Surely I have quieted myself, as a child that is weaned of his mother: my soul is even as a weaned child." The words mean that, by a simple trust in God, he was now detached from all earthly care. He had committed his all to God, while he rested in His will. "Rest in the Lord and wait patiently for Him; fret not thyself in any wise . . . ."

Paul touches on this spirit of detachment and acquiescence in God's will even more impressively. In one place he presents us, almost incidentally, with a list of his afflictions "for Christ's sake." And he speaks of the deeper distresses which might emerge in the future; but with him all was well. "I have learned in whatsoever state I am therewith to be content." The secret of his inner peace we find in his great affirmation, "I know whom I have believed and I am persuaded that He is able to keep that which I have committed unto Him against that day." All was in Christ's safe hand; nothing in his own. He was, therefore, weaned from the breast of care and worry, and from all preoccupation with the coming day.

There are those whose temperament or disposition stand as a barrier between them and this quiet confidence in God. An example of this we find in the home in Bethany where the Son of God was ever welcome. While Mary rested at the feet of her Saviour, her equally pious sister was distracted with domestic care. However legitimate her toil, and however worthy her motives, our Lord reminded her of the danger of letting the world and its cares deprive her of spiritual rest.

That our earthly cares may involve us in a very great danger may be inferred from our Lord's words where He warns us with regard to His coming to judge the world. "And take heed to yourselves lest at any time your hearts be overcharged with surfeiting, and drunkenness, and the cares of this life, and so that day come upon you unawares. For as a snare shall it come on all them that dwell on the face of the whole earth." Here "the cares of this life" stand side by side with the grosser evils of surfeiting and drunkenness. It is also through the cares of this world and the deceitfulness of riches that the good seed of the kingdom withers and dies in many lives.

When the Lord asks us to cast **all** our care upon Him at the throne of grace we are prohibited from classifying our cares into the smaller and the greater — those that we might be able to bear ourselves, and those under which the Lord only can help us. It was David who said, "I have put the Lord before me; and because He is at my right hand I shall not be moved." He never said, "This problem, this care, this trial is something which I can handle myself." No. With him God must always be at hand to help him every step of the way. "Without Me ye can do nothing." But "we can do all things through Christ who strengtheneth us." If unto His faithful hands we in faith commit ourselves and all our concerns we make the discovery that God cares for us infinitely more than we care for ourselves. So great indeed, is His care of us that it is extended to "the infinitesimals" of our lives. "The hairs of your head are all numbered." These words remind us of the minuteness of His providence, and that His love and care are extended to every part of our being and every detail of our life.

Our Lord has already given the greatest display of His love that we shall ever come to know. On the cross of Calvary He bore the burden of our sin and guilt. This burden He has put away "as far as the east is distant from the west." He has cast our iniquities into the depths of the sea. They are remembered no more. Intimately linked with that burden was the burden of our griefs and sorrows. "Truly He hath borne our griefs and carried our sorrows." Whatever burdens, therefore, are placed upon us for a moment here, they are, in the light of this great act of redemption and forgiveness, of little consequence. They are, in fact, like the touch of a feather compared to the burdens which lay on our soul in our state of condemnation, and which He, as our Substitute, bore on the tree.

Not only so, but all our "cares" are going to pass away like the blink of the eye. To use a simple illustration, let us for a moment stand before the mirror and blink our eyes. What happens? It is all over before it begins. The beginning and the end happen together. And all our sufferings here are, in their duration and measured by our eternal joy, a million times less than the blink of our eye! Is this not a sweet well of comfort to those whose souls are meantime discouraged because of the way? "For our light affliction, which is but for a **moment,** worketh for us a more abundant and eternal weight of glory."

Let me say another thing. Our Lord not only carries our burdens but He carries ourselves as well. Many years ago a gracious woman in the North of Scotland was on her death-bed. Her name was Marion MacLeod. The night before she died, and at her own request, a friend read out her favourite chapter. It was the sixty-third of Isaiah, where those often repeated and much loved words are to be found: "In all their afflictions He was afflicted, and the angel of his presence saved them: in his love and in his pity he redeemed them: and he bare them and he carried them all the days of old . . . . As the herd goeth down into the valley, the Spirit of the Lord caused him to rest; so didst thou lead thy people, to make thyself a glorious name . . . . Thou, O Lord, art our Father, our Redeemer: thy name is from everlasting." Listening to these words, and with the light of heaven already in her eyes, the dying woman whispered, "I shall not get all that I desire of that chapter till I enter eternity." "In love and in pity he redeemed them, and he bare them and carried them all the days of old." What we feel about these words is that every syllable emerges, as it truly does, from a depth of compassion beyond all knowledge.

The words also tell us of the eternal relationship in which He stands to all His people. "Verily thou art our Father." It was He Who, by a new birth and a gracious act of adoption, made them His own sons and daughters. Therefore they come to Him with all their needs and cares. This is their unspeakable privilege.

> "Such pity as a father hath,
>   Unto his children dear,
>   Like pity shows the Lord to such
>   As worship Him in fear."

Tomorrow, therefore, can bring us nothing but good, and fresh discoveries of His love and care. "Surely goodness and mercy shall follow me all the days of my life; and I will dwell in the house of the Lord for ever."

CHAPTER XII.

BROKEN TIES

ON that morning, as I walked through a Hebridean village, nothing could be heard but the subdued murmur of the western sea, the soaring notes of the skylark far up in the sky, and the sound of weeping in several homes which lay hard by the wayside. On that day trembling hands had opened letters conveying the sad tidings of the death of brave young sons who had fought and died for their country. Some could not weep, for the wells of grief were too deep for tears. In some of those homes there were devoted mothers and fathers who had been praying for their sons from the day they were born and who, in the day of peril, had committed them into God's strong hand. Some could rejoice in the hope that, through the saving grace of their Lord, their sons were now beyond all strife, and safe in their eternal Home. The tender ties of nature had been dissolved but, like a lighted candle in their hearts, a good hope through grace of a happy reunion in a better world enabled them to say "The Lord gave, and the Lord hath taken away; blessed be the name of the Lord."

Another boyhood memory is that of entering a home which had, a few months before, welcomed the arrival of a little child. Now he lay in the stillness of death. The young mother who met me at the door gave way to tears whenever she saw me. For several days before then I had called to ask for her ailing boy and to look wistfully and sadly into the cradle where he lay. In my own childlike way I suffered with her; but it was only when, many years afterwards, a similar sorrow had touched my own life, that I knew something of the anguish which lay within the stricken heart of that young mother.

More vivid than these memories is that of seeing another young woman standing with her head bowed at the door of her home. Her husband had recently died, and we all knew that a sense of great desolation filled her spirit. Their few years together were sweetened by the love of Christ. However, as she recalled his happy death-bed, and thought of their sure reunion in the Lord in that "city which hath foundations," and where death and sorrow are unknown, her sense of loneliness gave way to a deep peace which, she knew, would keep her heart and mind as long as she remained here.

In the experience of each one of us there may be memories quite as tender as these. What memories awake in our minds when, for example, we recall our last look at the dear face of a mother who invoked our first smile, to whose hand we clung, and to whose bosom we ran during the many falls and fears of our childhood days! We remember the prayer we first lisped at her knee. We may recall the prayers of a father who each day kneeled at the Throne of Grace and invoked God's blessing on his home and on his family. Blessed are all who can say as a result of their prayers and care, and when they are no longer here, "When my father and my mother forsake me, then the Lord will take me up."

Now these memories are not something merely human or sentimental. They weave themselves into our experience, and we know that, by God's grace, they are related to something of permanent value. To many death is just the end of all things. It hurts and grieves; but since it is a necessary law of all existence there is nothing to look for beyond the grave. We just move into the inevitable and eternal nothingness out of which we emerged. But such an outlook — alas! so common in our day — is a contradiction of God's Word, and of all Christian hope. It is, indeed, a contradiction of reality itself as it is apprehended by those whose inner eyes look at the things which are unseen and eternal. Grief, through the broken relationships of life, is as significant as it is real. So is the hope of all true believers by which they look beyond this vale of tears toward the day when God shall wipe away all tears from their eyes. The Bible is a true mirror of the fact that, in the midst of bereavements, God's people can look forward to the day when those "who died in the Lord" meet to part no more.

The deep pathos with which the Bible portrays both the grief and the hope associated with Christian bereavement is not without its strong consolation. For example, the answer of "the great woman" to the prophet's question with regard to her child, is full of hope and comfort. The child was God's gift to her for her kindness to His servant. But one day the child lay on her bosom and died. In her grief she sought the presence of her friend who asked her a question: "Is it well with the child?" And she answered, "It is well." What interpretation can we give to these words? The child **had** died. For a true and satisfying answer we must look at a phrase in the Epistle to the Hebrews where the faith of God's people in other ages is described in all its wonderful endurance, achievement and power. "Women received their dead raised to life again." By a miracle of God's power, exercised through the channel of faith and prayer, her child returned into her bosom alive. From the bosom of the Redeemer in heaven he returned to sweeten her earthly pilgrimage here for a little while. This instance of God's power was given to the Church of God as one sure proof, among many, that "it is well" with all who die in the Lord.

David's faith embraced the same great truth and comfort. When his ailing and beloved child breathed his last here, he ceased his prayer and put away the garments of his sorrow. He knew that, perfect and happy in the presence of God, his child was beyond both the need and the reach of his prayers. "I shall go to him, but he shall not return to me." His child had gone to God, and very soon he would join him in the great congregation above. Samuel Rutherford once wrote a friend who had laid her child in the grave: "She is not lost who is found in Christ. She is like a star which, though going out of sight, shines in another world. You should rejoice that you have now someone up in Heaven."

C. H. Spurgeon once preached a memorable sermon on the words which we have just quoted — "Is it well with the child?" Let me give one or two quotations. "Now, let every mother and father here present know assuredly, if God has taken your child away from you in its infant days, then all is well. You never heard its declaration of faith. It was not baptised in the name of the Triune God. It was not capable of giving that 'answer of a good conscience toward God.' Nevertheless, you may rest assured that, in a higher and better sense, it is well with the child — infinitely and eternally. The loss of the child, you say, is a heavy cross to carry. But we 'sorrow not as others which have no hope.' If you could only for a moment see your own child above and hear his sweet voice before the Throne of God, you would wipe away your tears."

On this subject the famous preacher, John Newton, expresses well the more common Reformed view in these words: "I am willing to believe, till the Scripture forbids me, that infants who died before they are capable of sinning 'after the similitude of Adam's transgression,' who have done nothing in the body of which they can give account, are included in the election of grace, and that the words of the Lord are also applicable to them, 'It is not the will of My Father in Heaven that one of these little ones should perish.' " All infants who belong to the election of grace — regenerated by the Spirit and accepted in Emmanuel's righteousness — are present with the Lord.

Such separations are often blessed to those who are left to mourn. "The best way to get a reluctant sheep into the fold is to carry its lamb there first." Many parents could trace the beginnings of their Christian interest and concern on the departure of their child. God can bless these bereavements in other ways also.

The story is told of an old Christian man who once found himself in the company of a stranger. They were both on the way to Communion services. The way was long, and when night came they entered a house where they were kindly received by a young man and his wife. But as they awoke in the morning they heard the sound of weeping; for the only child had died in the night. On the way home the old man was asked by his friend if he had seen anything which surprised him since he had left his home. "Yes," he said, "I was surprised at the Lord's hand in that home where we lodged for a night." "The young man and his wife," said his companion, "who received us so kindly in that home both know the Lord, but with the arrival of their child came a diminished interest in their spiritual duties and a cooling of their love to the Saviour. But the chastisement will yield its own blessing. It will also bring them nearer to the One who took their child to Himself."

One great danger to which we are exposed under the Lord's loving rod is to murmur at His dealings with us. Such a spirit can be destructive of our spiritual peace. A Christian lady used to tell her friends about her own father's love for a son who was lost in the First World War. This godly boy was the apple of his eye, and often did he express the wish that he might be again at his side; but he was led to see that his son, having tasted of the unfading joys of heaven, had no desire to return to our pained and sin-stricken world. From that hour his sorrow was turned into joy, for he knew that they would soon meet again in a better world.

When God tells us that all things work together for the good of those who love Him, our faith should rest in His promise. If, on the lap of grief, we cannot always discern how He can "bring meat out of the eater and sweetness out of the strong," we know, on the other hand, that with Him all things are possible.

In the North of Scotland there was an excellent minister of Christ who spent his earlier years in the happy companionship of a wife whose spiritual sympathies in all things coincided with his own. But in a moment she was taken from his side. The night his loved one was lying in the silence of her last sleep he prayed in the presence of his friends, "If," he said, "an angel from heaven had told me that this would work for my good I would not believe him; but since Thy Word says it, I must believe it." If all these ties are tender, are there not also other ties of real spiritual affection which bind us to our friends in the Lord? The love of Ruth to Naomi, and of David to Jonathan, was higher and deeper than that which exists within mere natural ties. The last chapter in the Epistle to the Romans is largely made up of apostolic "greetings" to friends in the Lord. The love of Christ is that which bound them all together in everlasting bonds. There are no final farewells; for they were all to meet again.

> "So part us sadly in this troublous world
> To meet again in sweet Jerusalem."

Many years ago two elderly men might be seen walking along a country road in our Scottish Highlands. They were both eminent men of God. For several days they had been attending Communion services, and now they were about to say a final farewell to one another till they would meet again. "And what word are you leaving with me as we now separate?" the one asked his friend. His companion replied by quoting the words of the Benediction: "The grace of our Lord Jesus Christ, and the love of God, and the communion of the Holy Ghost be with you. Amen." When these words were spoken his friend said, "Here, then, we shall meet no more." Then they parted each knowing that their next meeting would be where the great blessings inherent in those words would have their perfect and eternal fulfilment. God was about to undo the earthly tie that they might be bound with a more enduring bond in His own presence. And so it was.

One of the joys in store for God's people is the joy of meeting again those beloved friends who are, meantime, fallen asleep. This desire, like every other implanted in the soul by the Spirit of God, God shall satisfy.

We heard once of a good man whose dearest friend on earth was removed from his side. One evening he sat down in his home and he said, "Good were it for me if I were now with—" This remark was followed by a strange silence. His prayer was immediately answered. He was here no more.

The question of our mutual recognition in heaven has often perplexed some of God's people. The Scriptures everywhere imply that, as an obvious fact of existence, our recognition of one another there is certain. Our personal identity is something which remains with us forever. We shall be there in the likeness of Christ, and yet each one of His people shall preserve his or her own individual likeness. It is also of the nature of God's saving work to integrate, elevate and purify our beings. In Heaven, all our faculties shall function at their highest level, and since both the power of recognition and memory are essential aspects of man's nature it is impossible that we should not know each other there. And next to being with God, the best thing is to spend eternity with those He loved — and who are loved by us.

CHAPTER XIII.

"BY BABEL'S STREAMS"

NOT so long ago a medical practitioner told me of a friend who was under a heavy cloud of spiritual depression. He was a man who lived very near the Lord, and one who observed with deep concern those movements and tendencies within the visible Church which cannot but alarm every true Christian mind in our day. He was a mourner in Zion.

Such men and women have always, thank God, been in the world — especially in times of apostacy and spiritual decline. They are, on the other hand, a people whom the world derides. They are "the narrow-minded, puritanical type" who, in an age of greater ecclesiastical charity, refuse to move with the times. "A peculiar people," they are aware that the cause of their sorrow is something which can never touch the heart of those to whom God is a Stranger. They mourn because their prayers for the revival of God's diminished cause remain, for the time being, unanswered. They fear that their own unfaithfulness brings them under God's rebuke. They say with others of old:

> "O Lord of hosts, almighty God,
> How long shall kindled be —
> Thy wrath against the prayer made
> By Thine own folk to Thee."

These are truly a people who partake of the afflictions

of Christ and who have fellowship with Him in His sufferings. Their Lord Himself was a Weeper here. He wept over a people whom He would have gathered to Himself, but who rejected Him in His Person and Word. And the hour of His rejection, derision and death coincided with the unity of His enemies, both in the Church and outwith its pale. It was through His rejection and crucifixion that Pilate, Caiaphas and Herod became "friends."

Now the Scriptures teach that there is more than one way of crucifying Christ. Like the Church in Galatia we may do it by adding our own so-called "merits" and the traditions of men to the Righteousness of Christ and to the truth of His Gospel. The one excludes the other, for the two are opposed. When we add our own and contrary word to His, we crucify Him afresh. For the written and the incarnate Word are ultimately one and the same. Paul, in the blindness of his unbelief, "persecuted" Christ when he persecuted His people and sought to suppress the truth of the Gospel. Christ is so identified with His Word and people here that when we oppose the one we oppose the other. And this process is continuous. "For Thy sake we are killed all the day." "Ye have made the commandment of God of none effect by your tradition."

Perhaps the saddest part of the story is that those who have inflicted the greatest damage on the Church's life and witness have often been men who had been nursed in her own bosom. The false prophets of the days of Isaiah and Jeremiah were professedly her own sons. They were the "liberals" who compromised the truth of God. They made a God in their own image. He was a God who winked at evil. He was One in whom there

was no wrath, and One who would have all men live
in peace within a wide circle of "tolerance" and "charity."
The religion of the surrounding nations had their own
values. Baal, they claimed, could be worshipped as
well as the God of Israel. Each man could do "what
seemed right in his own eyes." Why not? Religious
freedom is the right of man. Could they not all agree
to differ — even in matters spiritual? So deep did this
process of degeneration become that many of God's true
prophets sighed out of their broken hearts.

But all this, one may say, happened long, long ago.
Are we not living in a different world today?

Historically speaking, it is, indeed, a far cry from
those days to our own. Since those days nations and
civilisations have come and gone. Thousands of generations have passed away "like a tale that is told." Prophecy
has been fulfilled at its highest level. Christ, "the Sun
of the Righteousness" and "the Desire of the nations"
has appeared in the fulness of times. He was in the
world. He died, rose again from the dead, and is now
exalted at God's right hand. His coming has finalised
God's Revelation of His mind and grace to mankind.
The Gospel of His grace is before us in the Bible in all
its fulness and perfection. He commanded that it should
be preached to all nations, for it is the only "power of
God unto salvation to all who believe." It is God's last
word to our sinful world, and as such we must not take
from it and add to it.

In the New Testament, on the other hand, we are
presented with awe-inspiring predictions and warnings
with regard to the evils which were to emerge in the
world and within the Church itself "in the latter days."
These days are spoken of as "perilous" in every sphere

of life. Christ spoke of the day when there would be world-wide departure from the faith of the Gospel. Deceptive cults and religions would arise in the world which, if that were possible, would deceive the very elect. Iniquity would abound, and the love of many, both for Himself and for His Gospel, would wax cold. Many false "prophets" would arise who would deny the faith, and who, by a parade of learning — using "great swelling words of vanity" — would lead many astray.

And all this has happened. Swarms of such "scholars", within the major Protestant denominations, are on the scene today. Whether we study the incoherent "concepts" of Barthianism, the "myths" and blasphemies of Bultman and Barclay, or the "Existentialism" of neo-orthodoxy, we are confronted with the same poisonous spiritual atmosphere — the disparagement and the denial of the truths of the Gospel. Prophecy is having its ominous fulfilment.

Along with this there is the dread prophetic picture of "the mystical Babylon" who "sits on many waters," and on the throne of which sits a man who exalts himself above what is called God. The person is described as "the anti-Christ" and "the man of sin." The Word predicted that this system was to develop, and to come to maturity, in the course of history.

The Reformers had no difficulty in identifying this system as the Roman Church. To a man like John Calvin, the Roman Church was "the masterpiece of Satan." Over sixty years ago an English bishop — Bishop Woodsworth of Lincoln — wrote a book in which he proved that nothing has appeared on the stage of history answering to this prophetic picture except the Roman Church. Some Roman Catholic scholars have been forced, in the light of all the evidence, to admit the validity of his conclusions.

And this is the so-called Church toward which an ever-rising stream of nominal Protestant denominations are moving with a view to achieve what is called "the union of Christendom." And the Roman Church is most accommodating! She has succeeded in putting on a "new look," so that all who are touched by the "unity" epidemic might find their way, in lowly submission, into her bosom. Her voice is now softer, and "the new reformation" which is supposed to be going on within her borders, has impressed many who fail to see that a true Scriptural reformation would involve her in self-destruction, since her dogmas, blasphemies, and doctrinal perversions are deeply contradictory of God's Word. Its exaltation of the creature, even above the Creator, marks it as a system which is not only un-Christian but anti-Christian. This is what is present, for example, in its Marian dogma and in the claim of the Pope to be the head of the Church.

What, we ask, lies behind this movement within the Protestant Churches? This is, indeed a question which would take long to answer; for the background of the whole movement is steeped in a major Protestant, or theological tragedy.

In my hand, for example, I hold a book. It was written by a typical liberal scholar of over half a century ago. The times were then quiet and optimistic. Modern science was still in its infancy, but even then new conceptions of man and of the world were taking shape. It had been "established," as the writer tells us, that man was not the "lost" being described in the older theology. Instead, he was an ascending creature who was slowly emerging out of his slough of despond into a state of moral righteousness, spiritual peace, and social security. The wars and conflicts which had bedevilled his lot in the past would soon, like a grim nightmare, be forgotten. Human nature was becoming "sweeter and sweeter." Besides all this a God of love was in His Heaven, and under his Fatherly smile the world was supremely safe.

In such a supposedly new and awakening world, an old-world book like the Bible, with its primitive conception of God and man, with its crude fears and threatenings, with its rigid laws and historical myths, must be examined afresh in the light of new discoveries and learning. A huge fierce wave of destructive criticism had already passed over it in Germany. The same was happening in America and Britain. It all ended, as we know, with the Holy Volume being denuded of its supernatural glory and its historical and doctrinal trustworthiness questioned at every turn.

This virtual rejection of the Bible within the major Protestant denominations created a wide spiritual and moral vacuum, which, in the nature of things, could not for long remain unoccupied. The kindly breezes of humanism and of scientific and "theological" optimism would, no doubt, blow in to fill this vast emptiness which the rejection of the Gospel had created.

This mirage, as we know, soon faded out in storms of war which, in dimension and duration, made all the wars of history look quite innocent. The deceptive voices of "peace, peace" were soon drowned amid the cries of a pained world. But the new type of ministry which by this time the new theology had brought into being looked upon this as the dying kick of "the animal" in man. They were men who had rejected "the fundamentalist

myth" of man's need of regeneration by the Spirit of
God. Humanity, they preached, was passing on through
its last dark patch towards the uplands of a new age.
Those billows belonged to the harbour leading into the
haven of peace.

But with an exhibition of cruelty without parallel in
the history of nations, in a country like Germany, with
a black atheistic curtain across half the world, and with
the arrival of the nuclear age these world churchmen
at last awoke to face reality. The world of their dreams
was shattered. They were gazing into an abyss, the
bottom of which none can see. They must do something
to save the nations from these unpredictable perils. Was
there a door of escape?

Would they call the nations back to the Word of God,
and tell them that only in a return to the Bible — God's
revealed will for man — was there any hope of salvation
and survival for man? Would they call the people to
repentance in the light of the great transgressions of the
age? This is what they should have done; but this is
what they would not do. To do these things would
involve them in "a loss of face," for this modern age.
It could not be done; for they were men with other
and bigger ideas.

The grand vision or the balm for an anxious and
apprehensive age was found in the idea of "one world,
one Church." Such a Church could stand as a bulwark
between us and the perils to which we were now exposed.
It could speak with a united and authorative voice to a
confused world.

Two inevitable questions arise here. The first is what
do we mean by the Church, and in what sense is it
united? Ultimately, of course, the Church, which is

invisible and known only to God Himself, consists of
all those whom God had chosen in Christ from everlasting.
They are the people for whom Christ died, who are
called out of death into life by His Spirit and justified
by the faith which is in Christ Jesus, and who are all
united in their Head, Jesus Christ. They are a people
who answer to the description which the Lord gives to
His own Church in the Gospel. Members of this Church
are found within every denomination which makes up
that visible Church which professes the true religion and
to which Christ has committed His Word, ordinances
and ministry. It is possible to be in the visible Church
and yet lack the supreme qualification for admission
into the invisible which is union with Christ through a
spiritual rebirth. The true Church is "the Church of
the first born written in heaven." The inescapable impera-
tive for membership in this Church is inherent in Christ's
words: "Ye must be born again."

What lends unity to the dispersed family of God in
the world is their union with Christ through spiritual
regeneration, and the fact that the Spirit of God who
dwells in them is infinite, and is therefore able to unite
them in the truth and in love to their Lord and to
one another. This love in the Truth, and for the Truth,
is the only unifying power in His Church. The true
Church of God we may, therefore, identify in the world
by her loving submission to God's will as revealed in
the Scriptures and by her unqualified acceptance of
the whole counsel of God. This was how the various
"Churches" of the apostolic age were united, and on
mere outward uniformity there was no insistence at all.
They kept "the unity of the Spirit in the bonds of
peace" while each congregation might remain autono-

mous and independent. This spiritual unity is the only unity Christ recognises. We might even say that members of the true Church of God within the different denominations may differ — as they did within the different churches of the Apostolic age — on many minute points; but they are entirely agreed on all the weightier matters of the faith for they are taught by the one Spirit. In the words of Bishop Ryle "Take three or four of them, strangers to one another, from the remotest corners of the earth; examine them separately on these points; you will find them all of one judgment."

The movement towards Rome is, needless to say, one which is moving further and further away from the Truth into the unrelieved darkness of error and confusion. One cannot help seeing that the enemy of God, aware that his time is short, is in a hurry to bring his dark designs within the visible Church to fulfilment. These men are also in a hurry. They have pin-pointed the year 1980 as the year which shall mark the consummation of all their efforts. But the Lord will act in His own time. If they only knew the terrors which are shortly to descend on our world they would remain silent. Their Tower of Babel He shall raise to the ground. Then His own weeping people shall be like those who dream. Meantime let us watch and pray and plead His promises, "for they that sow in tears reap in joy." "When the Lord shall build up Zion He shall appear in His glory. He will regard the prayer of the destitute and not despise their prayer."

At the bar of Scripture we believe that these storms shall coincide with her emergence out of her present danger, obscurity and enfeeblement. They shall prepare the way for her long period of renewal and peace when, embracing Jews and Gentiles, she shall be clothed with light, holiness and power. It has often happened in history that her increase, freedom and revival coincide with the downfall and destruction of those nations which sought her hurt and refused to serve her. It was so with Egypt, Moab, and Babylon in the ancient world. Those nations, on the other hand, which gave her a place in their bosom God blessed. The upheavals of this modern age are not, therefore, necessarily inimical to her welfare. They merely pave the way for her enlargement and spiritual prosperity. God shall answer her prayers "by terrible things in righteousness." There is nothing in Scripture more terrible than the picture it gives of the downfall of the Roman Church, the Great Babylon, and of the nations which advanced her power. "And the cities of the nations fell, and great Babylon came in remembrance before God to give unto her the cup of the wine of the fierceness of His wrath."

In Psalm forty-six, in which God commands us to exercise quiet confidence and faith in His power and faithfulness, we are given an awe-inspiring picture of the terrors and desolations which are to appear on the earth. The mountains, or the kingdoms of this world, disappear in the stormy sea of God's indignation. "The heathen raged, the kingdoms were moved. God uttered His voice, the earth melted." But in the midst of these upheavals God's river flows gently on. Its streams are undisturbed. They refresh, sustain and gladden God's city. Here is a picture of the true Church of God — unmoved and unmoveable — in the days of peril. God, who is in her midst, is her Helper. Whatever the physical devastations or political derelictions of the age, she is going to survive, and, in the garments of righteousness,

to carry on her warfare and maintain her witness to the
end of time. "Rejoice ye with Jerusalem, and ye that
mourn for her. For thus saith the Lord I will extend
peace to her like a river . . . . and ye shall be comforted
in Jerusalem."

CHAPTER XIV.

THE IMPERILLED WORLD

RECENTLY an American lady wrote in a widely-read Christian magazine about a discovery she made of the moral state of her own country. This lady had travelled in the Eastern world, and had visited cities and communities where the Christian religion had comparatively few followers. But on the streets of these cities she could walk at any hour of the night without fear of being molested. Not so in Washington? No woman could walk alone on many of its streets without a real danger of being molested by evil men who were on the prowl to waylay the unwary. The same could be said of many communities in our own land.

This, of course, is not a new thing. The "wicked," or the morally depraved, have always been in the world. Whatever degree of true godliness and Christian behaviour may exist among us, "the sons of Belial," are to be found in every generation. The Psalmist gives us such a vivid description of these that one would think he had lived to see and hear a "type" which is appearing on the scene in our own day. "They return in the evening: they make a noise like a dog, and go round about the city. Behold they belch out with their mouth; for who, they say, doth hear." The philosophy of "I couldn't care less," and the limited, incoherent vocabulary of the vandal element in society appear in these words.

It would, we thing, be wrong to deny that a "type" is emerging in society who express the dangerous tendencies and influences which are peculiar to our age. The age is one of material prosperity and "security." It also provides a continual riot of so-called pleasure for those who want it. And most people do! The wages we earn are given for the minimum of work. If this is seriously opposed a few strikes or threats usually bring the powers that be into the path of compromise and conciliation. With our material comforts there are media of entertainment which are deliberately debasing. Our television sets, for example, often portray life, not as it should be lived by God's prescribed standards, but at it lowest level. Crime, indecency, sexual perversion and all manner of lawlessness, are dramatised and made to appear "real" over this powerful means — to which the eyes of millions are glued for hours each day. And it is a proven phychological fact that of all our sense perceptions seeing makes a deeper impression on the mind, emotions and instincts than any other. Any respectable presentation of life put across by such means is no compensation for its involvement in the low, the foul and the unclean. Our printing presses also spew out their fictitious filth which, do what we will, reaches and is welcomed by large numbers of the masses. There are other sources of demoralization which one could mention. And because the heart of man is by nature "desperately wicked," and wholly unpredictable with regard to the extent to which it may go in the way of evil, its ready response to all these objective presentations of life on a low moral level cannot but fill us with alarm and fear.

Already we are confronted with moral problems of great magnitude. Many live without any knowledge of God, or any standard of morality. There are others who

are shameless in the more perverted relationships, and
many in places of influence both in Church and State are
not ashamed to advocate that the sins of Sodom shall,
in law, be recognised. And the solemn question arises:
will these trends continue and increase till our Lord's
prophetic words have their fulfilment? Since, apart from
the power of God, there is no power on earth that can
arrest this flood it can only increase. "For as in the
days that were before the flood, they were eating and
drinking, marrying and giving in marriage, until the
day that Noah entered into the ark, and knew not until
the flood came and took them all away." . . . . "Know this
also, that in the last days perilous times shall come . . . ."
Have these days arrived? Are we about to reach the
point of no return, where our transgressions are making
contact with the Judgment of God? The nuclear age is
here. The inescapable shadow, more terrible than any
that ever appeared in history, is already over our world.

An ominous charactertistic of our age is the way in
which those who should try to preserve the moral foundation of society, are trying to adapt themselves to these
unwholesome trends. It is not, with these men, what
God commands, but what "public opinion" calls for.
Is the Sabbath law — to use but one example — too
"narrow" and restrictive for this modern age? Then let
it be changed and relaxed. And in contrast to this, little
or nothing is said about the many millions of money
being spent on such destructive habits as drunkenness
and gambling.

This, then, is the kind of world in which God's people
find themselves today. And what can they do? Apart
from their Christian witness they can do nothing. They
can also, as a matter of Christian duty, pray and wait

upon God that He might arise to plead His own cause in the earth.

Let me, at this point, mention an experience which came my way a short time ago. I was, at the time, under a heavy burden of concern over the state of the world, and of God's cause. I asked God if there was anything His people could do in such an hour. A few nights afterwards He answered my prayer in the words of a Psalm: "If the foundations be destroyed, what can the righteous do?" One exact expositor says that these words are one of the funeral sermons of the Church of God, or are like "the last bell" before the ship sinks. What can we do? We can only bow our heads in awe and wait for God to do His strange work. "The Lord is in His holy temple, the Lord's Throne is in heaven. His eyes behold, His eyelids try the children of men." And what does He see? A foul, contaminated world which must be purged by fire. "Upon the wicked he shall rain snares, fire and brimstone, and an horrible tempest. This shall be the portion of their cup."

The foundations mentioned in the Psalm do not, of course, mean the ultimate spiritual foundations on which the true Church of God rests. These are eternal and unmovable. Christ, the eternal Son of God, is the Rock against which the gates of hell cannot prevail. His unchanging infallible Word is another foundation which cannot be moved. On Him and on His Word the faith of His people rests for ever. And so it is written "the foundations of the Lord standeth sure, having this seal, the Lord knoweth them that are His." The words of the Psalm refer to the "pillars" or foundations of the social and political order. These, through spiritual degeneration and moral corruption, disintegrate and fall asunder. The righteous are helpless in such a situation, for they see not only that "the foundations of the earth are out of joint" but that God Himself is about to arise "to shake terribly the earth."

But whatever our conscious helplessness we must not deviate from the path of duty. The Lord has commanded us to watch and pray. "And that, **knowing the time**, that now it is high time to awake out of sleep."

Even when we know that the Judge is at the door we should, like Abraham before the destruction of Sodom, continue to wrestle with God for the preservation of His cause and people. We should, like Habbakuk, pray, not that His judgments may pass us by, but that He would revive His work, and in wrath remember mercy.

What, in such an hour, should be our Christian attitude, and what are the sources of our comfort? Our attitude, indeed, should be one of acquiescence in the sovereign will of God. He commands us to be still and to know that He is God. "Shall not the Judge of all the earth do right?"

God's people, like Moses and the prophets, may tremble as they hear His voice; but however much it may shake the heavens and the earth it is still the voice of the Beloved.

An excellent Christian woman stood one night in the door of her home listening to the loud reverberating thunder which rolled over the face of the deep. "Are you not afraid standing out there on such a night?" someone asked her. "Why," she answered, "should I fear; for I am listening to my Father's footsteps." Therefore, because it is He Who is passing by "we will not fear though the earth be removed."

Is it not also a source of great comfort to every

believer to know that the history of the Church of God is replete with instances of God's care for His people in the midst of calamities. And His gracious, and often miraculous, interventions are continuous. In such an age let us hide ourselves in the secret of His presence where no harm can befall us. "When thou liest down, thou shalt not be afraid: yea, thou shalt lie down, and thy sleep shall be sweet. Be not afraid of sudden fear, neither of the desolation of the wicked, when it cometh."

We remember how, during the Cuban crisis, the earth stood still for fear. As the nations moved toward "the brink," everything on the human plane seemed remote and irrelevant. Eternity became a terrible reality. At that time, many wrestled with God in prayer that He might restrain the wrath of man and shield His own cause and people in a catastrophic age. And here let me mention a strange experience I had at that time. One night I retired to rest after a season of prayer. And then I dreamed. I found myself sitting beside a serene and holy-looking man whom I had never seen in this world. The theme of our conversation was God's care of His people in every age — so vividly portrayed in the Psalm: "He suffered no man to do them wrong: yea He reproved kings for their sake, saying, Touch not mine anointed and do my prophets no harm." When shortly afterwards the news of God's intervention reached us we knew that, without His permissive will, no man can move a finger, and that the preservation of His people is something very dear to the heart of God. The storm is yet to come, but whatever may happen, our life — in the highest and ultimate meaning of that word — is hid with Christ in God.

"As the mountains are about Jerusalem so is the

Lord round about his people from henceforth even for ever." In His eternal purpose of grace; in all His attributes, reconciled to them through the blood of the covenant, and in the processes of His Providence, He surrounds them night and day. "He that dwelleth in the secret place of the Most High shall abide under the shadow of the Almighty."

"In the shadow of thy wings will I make my refuge, until these calamities be overpast."

CHAPTER XV.

THE LAST ENEMY

A FAMOUS preacher once said that there were golden hours in the lives of many of God's people when they could, without fear, look beyond the trials of this life, the grave, and even their final judgment before God, to the day when they would see their Lord face to face. Perfect love casts out fear and makes little of these awesome events which stand between it and the One on whom it rests. Like Moses on the top of Pisgah, there are days when, by a clearer faith, they see the King in His beauty in the land of far distances. In such seasons they look, without fear, beyond the narrow stream which all must cross. These hours, however, do not last. The old fears may often return.

There are many, indeed, who through fear of death are all their lifetime subject to bondage. For one thing "nature has an instinctive dread of its own dissolution." There is also that deeper characteristic of our mind whereby we cannot as creatures made in the image of God, and partakers of His breath, conceive of ourselves as not being in existence.

But the Lord's people stand in awe of death for deeper reasons than these. They know that it marks the end of all privilege and of the day of grace, and that time is given to be redeemed in the interests of eternity. God's Word tells them that "as the tree falleth so it shall lie," and that Death bears all who die unprepared down to endless grief. This fills them with concern.

In the Scriptures they read of the spotless purity of those who are in heaven — the place where love is perfected and where holiness is the air which its inhabitants breathe. "There shall in no wise enter in anything that defileth or worketh abomination or maketh a lie." One evil thought or desire, one sinful stain, one root of resentment or ill-will, would be enough to exclude them from these realms of glory. While they seek to prepare themselves for that holy world, as God commands, they know that they must be prepared by God Himself, and that the imperatives of Heaven cannot be by-passed. Those who are there are born again. They are clothed in the best robe of Emmanuel's righteousness. They are washed in His blood and perfected by the indwelling of the Holy Spirit. When, in the light of all this, they examine their lives and hearts, they bow their heads and say with another, "In me, that is in my flesh, there dwelleth no good thing." They feel unprepared, but death cannot be delayed.

> "I am on the brink of Jordan;
> Backward shrinks this mortal frame;
> Well 'twere now for me to have
> The hope that ne'er shall put to shame."

That is not the concern of those whose fears are merely slavish or "natural." On the other hand, it is far removed from the false hope and deceptive peace of "Mr Bad-Man" and "Ignorance." The one died like a lamb, while the other was ferried across the river by his own Vain Hope. "There were no bands in their death."

God's people differ from such in that all their hope is centred in Christ. Their hope and interest rest in what He is, on what He has promised, on what He did and on what He is yet to do. He is the eternal Son of God who died in their nature to redeem them. It is derived from the knowledge and assurance that they are identified with Him in His redemptive work. His death was their death. His life is the abiding guarantee of their everlasting salvation. On the Cross of Calvary death left its sting in His soul. He died that they might live. The power which wrought in Him when God raised Him from the dead is the same power that is exerted in their salvation. That power lies behind their spiritual resurrection, their preservation and their appearance in His presence. "I give them eternal life and they shall never perish neither shall any man pluck them out of My hand." "They are kept by the power of God through faith unto salvation ready to be revealed at the last time. To experience God's saving and keeping power in our own lives should provide us with the assurance that neither death nor life is able to separate us from His love. Our union with Him is untouched by whatever may happen. The grave is but one of the chambers where Christ's Bride, in her mortal frame, sleeps for a while. At His coming again she shall awake satisfied in His likeness.

On his death-bed Jacob speaks of his desire to be with God. "The God of Bethel" was the Angel who fed him, who kept him and who led him, all his days. Now as the end of his earthly pilgrimage draws near he expresses the longing that had been, we believe, in his heart ever since that wistful morning when, on the slope of Bethel, God blessed him. "I have waited for thy salvation, O Lord." Having said this, "he was gathered to his people." He was not really to die but to live. The God of Jacob — as our Lord reminds us — is not the God of the dead but of the living. God was Jacob's Friend in the house of his pilgrimage. Now he was to be gathered to His God in the Home above. "Gather my saints together unto me, those who have made a covenant with me by sacrifice." Death to God's people is, therefore, a moving out of this tabernacle into "the house not made with hands, eternal in the heavens."

A few nights ago I read the words of a young Scottish sailor who was lost in the Second World War. The Lord, by His Word, had been striving with this lad's soul, reminding him of the uncertainty of life and his need of salvation in Christ. This led him to seek the Lord at the Throne of Grace, and the Lord whom he sought heard his prayer. Shortly afterwards, he wrote to a friend telling him of the night his soul entered into peace. "One night, when on the look-out, I heard the Lord's voice speaking to me with power. "Gather my saints together unto me; those that have made a covenant with me by sacrifice." For the rest of the night I felt as if I were talking to my Saviour face to face. Two hours on the look-out after that, in the middle of the night, passed too quickly . . . . I have a small room to which I go for secret prayer and many a happy meeting I have with Him there. Indeed, I can often say in this room 'A day in thy courts is better than a thousand.'" The words through which this lad of twenty years was led into a state of grace had another and a higher meaning. In a few days the ship was struck down and he was gathered into the presence of the One whose Word had healed him. This, then, is the meaning of death. We are "gathered" Home.

Not only are the spirits of just men gathered to God, but their flesh rests in hope. Our bodies rest in the grave till the resurrection day. A mother, for example, puts her child to bed, kisses it goodnight, and gently withdraws the light. Sleep takes over, and nothing more is remembered till the same loved voice is heard in the morning. In the same way the Lord "gives His beloved sleep," till by the touch of His power and the sound of His voice they awake to see Him face to face. In that bed he lay Himself, and He left it warm and fragrant for all His loved ones. In the stillness of the grave their bodies are as near to Him as their souls before the Throne. He died to redeem both. He has the keys to death. When He broke through the gates of death He took possession of its keys. Death can never, therefore, retain any of those for whom He died and for whom He lives.

In the light of all this how significant are the words of David:

> "I will both lay me down in peace
> and quiet sleep will take;
> Because thou only me to dwell
> in safety, Lord, dost make."

A man once said that if, like Enoch and Elijah, he had the choice of entering heaven without seeing death or to enter it by way of the grave, he would rather choose the latter. He would choose this way because by it the Lord Himself and all the rest of the redeemed came and shall come to their everlasting rest and reward.

But however much we may reassure ourselves that "to die is gain" we still fear the day when we must leave this world. Although all our desire is before God, we are still conscious of "the plague of our heart." Therefore we fear that Death may find us unprepared. A true man of God was asked on his death bed how he felt, now that he was about to leave this world. His answer was "I can say that I was never more satisfied with God than I am now, and never was I less satisfied with myself." By these words he carried the earnest of eternal holiness in his heart.

The good Doctor Love of Greenock had a Christian lady in his congregation whose growing sense of sin often brought her into the depth of discouragement. Heaven, she would say, was not for her. Then the Lord took her Home. When her friend heard of the news of her departure, he remarked on the surprise she must have felt when she found herself in heaven! He knew that her constant cry after a clean heart was but the earnest of the glorious liberty of God's children. "The Lord," said David, "will perfect that which concerneth me." A famous preacher once said that God's child would carry in his bosom a sense of sin to the very last second of his life here; but that a billow of God's holiness would, in the moment of his departure, bear away for ever every stain and every remnant of corruption in his soul. Death shall then be swallowed up in life, and night in day.

The fear of death was often very real to an elderly Christian lady I once knew. Before she died she had her sister write me what must have been, I believe, her last letter. She wanted to tell me of an experience she had had a few nights before when she felt Death coming toward her on silent feet. As she stood in His presence she quoted the words of a Psalm:

> "Before me still the Lord I set;
>   Sith it is so that he
> Doth ever stand at my right hand
>   I shall not moved be.

> Because of this my heart is glad
>   And joy shall be exprest
> Ev'n by my glory; and my flesh
>   In confidence shall rest."

As these words fell from her lips her adversary seemed to retire. All fear left her for ever, for Christ was so near her. Death was given her to conquer. In a few days she was taken Home.

Many of God's people have been known to have lost all fear just when death knocked at their door. God's love and presence were then so real to them that their fears were banished. In this land of Beulah they enjoyed the beginnings of an endless day. They were conscious of a final detachment from "things seen."

Not long ago, in the north of Scotland, there was a young woman to whom the Lord had revealed that her season of illness would coincide with her departure out of this world. Her bands were untied. Her hope of seeing her Lord face to face filled her with deep consolation. But her illness seemed to pass away, and she wondered whether she had mistaken God's time and promise. One day she stood in the door of her home deep in thought. The raw edge of a cold wind penetrated her lungs and within a few hours she was in the land of her desire — "with Christ which is far better."

Another young Highland girl, "Cathie" Macrae — whose brief, broken but fragrant life is told in the book **My Beloved,** — had a visit from a friend some time before she died. In conversation she mentioned that the last fond link between her and everything here below had now been dissolved. Then she quoted the famous stanza:

"In peace let me resign my breath
  And Thy salvation see,
My sins deserve eternal death,
  But Jesus died for me."

When we die our souls immediately pass into glory. "Absent from the body we are present with the Lord."

Some of God's people have been able to tell a little of what they saw, and what took possession of their consciousness, in the hour of their departure, Stephen, Doctor Payson, Samuel Rutherford, and many others, have spoken of the bliss of Heaven while they were still breathing here. This, however, is the exception rather than the rule. The glories and the joys which embrace the soul then are so astonishing that the mind, in the enfeeblement of our earthly frame, cannot go into reverse to relate what it enjoys and sees. It is carried forward by all the amazing wonders which open before it. The soul is then utterly detached from all that is earth-bound. It has, as it were, taken a forward leap into the dimension of eternity. To speak, therefore — even if we could — of what we see and enjoy becomes a spiritual impossibility. We are wholly and eternally embraced. The same holds true of the lost. The fearful terrors which then engulf Christless souls carry them beyond the possibility of any further contact with this world. Many of those have, indeed, spoken of the terrors which held them. Those who speak flippantly about the fact that the dying are often silent, as a proof that death ends all, should take these solemn reflections into consideration. The rare testimonies of the dying with regard to eternal realities are consistent with God's Word in every case. In the mouth of such witnesses the Truth of God is established.

This is the hour in which we take leave of all our earthly friends. But for God's people there is no loneliness in death — others take the place of the friends who accompany us so far on this side. "But He is with us still." He is very near to us then. "This God is our God for ever and ever; He will be our Guide even unto death." These words, in their original meaning, assure us that He will not only guide us to death, but over death, and into the place where death in unknown.

Are there not others with us then also? Those ministering spirits who keep watch over us in all our ways here, accompanying us to the portals of bliss. These, as we have said before, are the heavenly guardians who surround the Bride of Christ, in all her members till she reaches her Home above. But the best of all is that we are in the arms of our Beloved and our Friend.

"Yea though I walk in Death's dark vale
    Yet will I fear none ill,
For Thou art with me and Thy rod
    And staff me comfort still."